The Future of Identity

The Future of Identity

Centennial Reflections on the Legacy of Erik Erikson

Edited by Kenneth Hoover

LEXINGTON BOOKS
Lanham • Boulder • New York • Toronto • Oxford

LEXINGTON BOOKS

Published in the United States of America
by Lexington Books
An imprint of The Rowman & Littlefield Publishing Group, Inc.
4501 Forbes Boulevard, Suite 200, Lanham, Maryland 20706

PO Box 317
Oxford
OX2 9RU, UK

Portions of chapter 8 appear in *The Hand of Compassion: Portraits of Moral Choice during the Holocaust*, published by Princeton University press, 2004.

British Library Cataloguing in Publication Information Available

Library of Congress Cataloging-in-Publication Data

The future of identity : centennial reflections on the legacy of Erik Erikson / edited by Kenneth Hoover.
    p. cm.
  ISBN 0-7391-0802-6 (hardcover : alk. paper) — ISBN 0-7391-0803-4 (pbk. : alk. paper)
  1. Identity (Psychology) 2. Erikson, Erik H. (Erik Homburger), 1902– I. Hoover, Kenneth R., 1940–
BF697.F88 2004
150.19'5'092—dc22   2004004986

Printed in the United States of America

♾™ The paper used in this publication meets the minimum requirements of American National Standard for Information Sciences—Permanence of Paper for Printed Library Materials, ANSI/NISO Z39.48–1992.

To Erik Erikson,

honoring

the centennial of his birth

Contents

Chapter One

Introduction:
The Future of Identity

Kenneth Hoover
Lena Klintbjer Ericksen

As the post-9/11 world witnesses the terror and warfare provoked by people's injured sense of who they are, how they are regarded, and what they deserve, we have entered into the "age of identity." Identity has become a critical category of political analysis, rivaling even economic self-interest in its potency. The headlines are filled with stories of those who sacrifice their well-being and their very lives to tell the world that they demand respect for their beliefs, communities, and ways of life.

Erik Erikson (1902–1994) was the prophet of this new age. Erikson's lifetime of clinical and interdisciplinary work on human development centered on the formation and maintenance of identity among people of diverse backgrounds: black, white, and Native American; rich, middle class, and poor; male and female. In this volume, we will describe his legacy and explore the challenges that the desire for identity brings to the contemporary world. We will also see where Erikson's work fits in with contemporary research on identity.

A century after his birth, and a decade after his passing, a powerful current of research carries the analysis of identity into a world torn between globalization and cultural particularism. These chapters show who Erikson was (Coles, Friedman), how his work was tested by empirical research (Marcia, Kroger), and what applications can be made to the vexing challenges of individual choice (Monroe), democratization (Hoover), globalization (Kinnvall), and Islamic fundamentalism (Kreidie).[1]

Before engaging these diverse perspectives on identity relations research, however, it is important to clear away some rival conceptions of identity that have gained currency in contemporary politics and scholarship. The preliminary task is to make clear what these chapters are *not* about so that the discussion can be placed securely on the foundation of the research and exploration fostered by Erikson's work. Then we turn to a synthesis of the conception of identity that emerges from empirical work in social psychology—and to some of the critics of this work. With this in mind we can preview the contributions of each of the authors of this volume.

Rival Theories of Identity:
Constructionists, Essentialists, and Individualists

What is identity? What is it made of? Where does it come from? The term is freely used as if everyone shares a common definition. Yet a sampling of current works illustrates that there is very little agreement about what identity is or what its connections are to politics and society. Or, rather, there is agreement *within* schools of scholars—and much disagreement *between* schools.

Three contemporary schools compete for favor. I will identify each of these schools and sketch their respective frameworks without naming names—of persons. There is the *constructionist* school where identity is seen as an artifact of power, or, more broadly, as the work of social forces. For the most extreme social constructionists, identities are created to serve the purposes of dominant interests and are visited upon people who do not have the power to resist. Second, there is the *essentialist* school, for whom identity is fixed by gender, race, and sometimes class. Each person is tied to their social and/or genetic origins. Finally, there is the *individualist* school in which identity is seen as self-created, as chosen, or as a matter of "affinity." The self-inventing "I" becomes the center of identity formation. These three reductionist positions are often modified in application, but, for the moment, it is instructive to examine the difficulties encountered by each perspective in pure form.

Each of these schools runs into its contradictions and its critics. Without rehearsing the literature, it is perhaps sufficient to point to the contradictions with everyday observation. For the constructionist school, there are the troubling cases of those whose identities are palpably formed in opposition to social forces. The courageous critic, the intrepid scholar, the resistance leader, the innovator, even the entrepreneur seem to escape—or at least stretch—the bonding forces by which, it is theorized, identity is shaped and molded. It is readily apparent that identity is both influenced by and resistant to power and social construction. The marionette is yanking on the strings even while dancing.

The essentialist school points to the immutability of gender, of ethnicity and race, of class origins, and even of religion. To the despair of those who would put the world together, the essentialists seem to take it apart. All the creations of modernism are threatened by their analysis. Apart from "us," there is no "we" to act with. Yet the impartial observer might notice that identity doesn't fit into these essentialist pigeon holes very often, or with notable constancy. In some situations race, for example, is of life and death significance in defining identity. However, on the job, race may not matter when the focus is on the task at hand. At home, another aspect of one's identity may surface—nurturer, autocrat, provider—come to mind. Clearly there is a social contextual term to identity that has us changing partners in our daily walk with destiny.

From the individualist vantage point, I am seen to be busy about choosing who I am today, or who I will be tomorrow. The celebrated "I" of Western philosophy appears in a leading role. The memory of existentialist philosophy informs this discussion. Individuals are seen to select affinities from among the essential and the notional aspects of their personhood. Yet, for all the assertiveness and choosiness of identity-related behavior, there is much observable shaping going on. That, after all, is the intentional project of education, democratic deliberation, and governance.

Each of these schools thus encounters obvious problems. The constructionists, in view of ordinary human experience, are too determinative and disabling of the impulse to personal agency. They often wind up as cultural relativists with little guidance to offer in the difficult choices individuals and societies must make. By the same test, the essentialists appear to be fatalists who fragment a world that needs and often finds commonality and mutual understanding. For the individualists, there is no system for finding the boundary between what can and cannot be changed, let alone for finding others to do the changing with.

For the advocate of democracy, there is trouble in all three schools. Both the constructionists and the essentialists offer fundamentally determinist perspectives that belie the promise of democratic change. If identity cannot be changed by our own exertions or if, on the other hand, identity is purely a matter of genetic or socioeconomic endowment, there is little prospect of common democratic action to alter the human condition. The individualists, while they contribute greatly to the discussion of democratic rights, lead the discourse away from the commonalities that resolve differences on issues of public policy. If identity arises only from impulses in our deepest selves and is unaffected by shared experiences, then democracy is largely a waste of time.

Identity Relations: An Observation-Based Conception

The problems of the rival schools are quite apparent to the naked eye. That is why these schools are so contestable on the grounds of common sense. Perhaps the reason for these afflictions lies in a common characteristic of *all* of these schools. Their advocates pay little or no attention to a stream of empirical research on identity formation that has occupied an interesting set of psychoanalysts and social scientists for the last half century.[2] This book illustrates what has been missed because of such inattention and amnesia.

Beginning in the 1940s, Erik Erikson pioneered a synthesis of psychoanalysis, social psychology, anthropology, and sociology in the course of coming to terms with the phenomenon of human identity. Erikson's work was taken up rather famously by Carol Gilligan, who sought out the differential impact of gender roles on identity development.[3] At the same time, and less famously, James Marcia, along with Jane Kroger and colleagues in many other universities, established the validity of identity as a theoretical construct usable in empirical research. In the course of interviewing thousands of people from a variety of cultural backgrounds and circumstances, they assembled a picture of the constituent elements of identity. By systematic use of a standardized interview protocol over the last thirty years in widely divergent settings, Marcia, Kroger, and their associates have demonstrated the empirical power of Erikson's formulation, while adding a dimension that is consistent with Gilligan's feminist perspective.[4]

Taken together, these streams of research have yielded remarkably convergent findings. I will summarize this research and focus on its meaning for politics. *What, then, is an identity?* The common sense answer is that it has to do with who we—and others—think we are. But what does that consist of? When asked who we are, the research shows, most of us will respond with:

> **What one does**—skills, vocations, roles (***competencies***)
> **Where one is from**—locations, beliefs, groups (***communities***)
> **Who one is with**—personal relationships (***commitments***)
> —or, in Erikson's term, *mutualities*

These three dimensions of identity vary widely, of course, in content. But the dimensions themselves do not vary appreciably.[5]

Competencies may reflect what one does for a living or perhaps a particular talent. Often in the next breath we try to put some credibility behind our claims. We can't just assert competence. We have to make others believe it. To claim to be a poet is to invite the question—where have you published? Competence is established when ability is matched by social legitimation and formal certification. The competence element of identity is a matter of ability and motivation—and, among the educated, of degrees duly conferred.

The *communities* that comprise identity for an individual are often taken to be the whole meaning of identity in contemporary social science.

Here we find the familiar markings of gender, race, ethnicity, class—but there are many more: religion, ideology, social groupings, and loyalties to country, school, and team. Again, it is hard to assert a community relationship without some sign of acceptance by other members. Wear the colors, yes; but walk the talk. Eat—and cook—the food.

Erikson's work also demonstrated the importance to identity of mutualities between persons. Carol Gilligan emphasizes the critical nature of these relations in the lives of women. The empirical research of James Marcia, Jane Kroger, and their colleagues affirms for both women *and* men that these interpersonal *commitments* are essential elements of identity. We are known to ourselves and others as spouses, partners, children, kith and kin, colleagues, and comrades. When reciprocated, and even when not, these commitments are critical to identity.

These therapists and researchers located the dimensions of identity the hard way: by treating children, young people, and mature adults who were missing something, or who were unable to locate themselves in some critical respect. The investigations of Erikson, Gilligan, Marcia, and Kroger revealed the *relational* nature of identity. None of the elements of identity is purely a matter of individual assertion, just as none of them is entirely given by our surroundings. Identity resides on the middle ground between what we bring from inner resources, and what society offers through its institutions, customs, and policies. For this reason, the approach taken here may be termed *identity relations analysis*.

The individual side and the social side of identity relations have to be viewed interactively. The social side, at least, can be altered and directed by deliberate cooperative action. Whether or not the societal dimensions of identity relations are subject to directed intelligence, they have their impact. Identity is not optional. People will act on their promptings toward identity in whatever theater is available.

To return to the contesting schools, neither essentialists nor constructionists have it completely right. Each element of identity is formed in a relation between native endowment and social response as mediated by an ever active psyche that struggles to put the best face on a sometimes confusing set of somatic promptings and social responses. In a manner pleasing to individualists, the ego does its work, albeit more by the negotiation and mediation of bounded relations than by choices freely made. Autonomy is an unnatural pose.

To summarize, identity relations are best captured by the image of a three-legged stool. To be firmly seated—and grounded—in relations of competence, community, and commitment is to have an identity. A broken leg requires leaning harder on the remaining two pins. Where I live in the Pacific Northwest, for example, there are displaced workers from the fields, factories, and forests whose competencies are no longer salable in the marketplace. In this unforgiving world that means they haven't the wherewithal to meet their personal commitments. So, some of them have a community of militia-styled, well-armed brothers who are very sure of one thing—that they, and their kind, are better than *them*. Such an oppositional worldview drives them to authoritarianism. They don't have much use for democracy. Identity becomes as much about the negation of the other as the affirmation of the self. In each of these chapters we will find insights into how societies can nurture developmentally secure and socially productive forms of identity and avoid the resort to extremism.

In the pages that follow we will see that Erikson's conceptual legacy is a good deal richer and more varied than the simple image of a three-legged stool can convey. Yet there are recurring themes of competency, community, and commitment throughout his work—and his life. With these themes in hand, we can begin this journey with Erikson's companions, protégés, followers, biographers, interlocutors, and his critics. A word about the latter will conclude this discussion.

Erikson and the Psychologists

Within the discipline of psychology, Erikson's theory has often been criticized for its lack of clear definitions and relative lack of testability.[6] This negative evaluation of Erikson's work arises from the desire among psychologists for explanations of behavior that rely upon measurable variables. What cannot be measured and subjected to statistical analysis is excluded from consideration. Given our limited powers of observation, several classes of behavioral influences fall outside this approach. The cultural context in which the individual lives, the dynamic interplay of elements of identity as described above, and the longitudinal integration of present and prior influences are all virtually impossible to measure by these means. Such aspects as language, behavioral norms, and specific historical events cannot easily be captured in operationalized definitions.

Consequently, Erik Erikson's concern for a psychohistorical approach—in which he emphasizes the unique cultural circumstances (encompassing political, economic, social, and linguistic forces) that shape an individual's development—is viewed with suspicion within the context of the traditional psychological paradigm. Additionally, Erikson's reliance on what many psychologists regard as arbitrary definitions and terms, such as identity and integration, renders his work, by their view, unnecessarily complex or, inversely, lacking parsimony.

Ironically, the statistical paradigm upon which such weight is placed in determining the validity of any given finding also has its own inherent limitations of applicability. However, these limitations are frequently ignored by the advocates of such methodology. Specifically, identity happens to individuals one at a time; yet psychology proceeds by observing patterns in large populations in order to achieve statistical validity. As in physics, in which much can be accurately stated about the average behavior of a large number of subjects (in the case of physics, particles), nothing can be accurately stated about the behavior of a particular individual (in physics, the definite motion of a single particle). This view of behavior based upon probability must acknowledge the fundamental uncertainty at the heart of all findings.

Erikson's theory respects this inherent "fuzziness" in the nature of evaluating behavior. His theory does not specifically predict how a given individual will resolve a particular developmental crisis; rather, his theory indicates that, as a member of a particular cultural context, a given individual is likely to approach such crises within certain boundaries of action.

The seemingly arbitrary terms Erikson employs to delineate his theory of development are not drawn from purely abstract constructs. The concepts he describes through the nomenclature of his theory come from the very fabric of human culture and often date back to the origins of civilization—identity, integrity, faith, culture. Surely, the concept of identity formation as Erikson understood it would be obvious to any citizen of ancient Greece. The universality of his ideas is apparent also in their applicability to cultures that are not informed by the Western cultural legacy. Indeed, a significant part of Erikson's field work was among Native American tribal cultures. Erikson's reliance on a variety of distinct cultures is what insures the relevance of his theory in a time of increasing recognition of cultural plurality.

Perhaps it is this quality of Erikson's work, in which he describes the stages of human development within a psychohistorical structure, that so defies the normative view of mainstream psychological doctrine. Rather than focusing on aspects of the human psyche that are readily quantifiable, Erikson based his work upon those parts of the human psyche that are culturally understood to be relevant. Out of this quality come the universality and extra cultural applicability of his work. Erikson was not seeking to understand only the workings of the European psyche; his realm of study was all of humanity.

The empirical validation found in the works of Marcia, Kroger, and others respects the parameters of the phenomenon of identity by looking at categories of identity elements. While the content within these categories may vary widely by culture, age, and stage, it is the striking consistency of the categories themselves that provides a universal framework for comprehending the human experience of identity. Analysis of this kind may not fit the criteria of higher levels of measurement; however the question is whether the phenomenon is more important that the tools used to measure it.

A Foretaste: Authors and Perspectives

For all the neatness of the categories that characterize Erikson's theory of identity, we have here a complex story to tell. For one thing, Erikson's full theory of the eight stages of human development is about much more than identity. However, for the full story, the reader needs to read Erikson himself. Here we will use identity as a thread to follow through a mosaic of impressions, research results, applications to contemporary politics, and ideas about the future. But first, we shall meet Erik and Joan Erikson.

Our examination of the "future of identity" begins with the past and two portraits of the founder of this tradition of research, Erik Erikson. Child psychiatrist Robert Coles was Erikson's close associate at Harvard. Inspired by Erikson, Coles went on to write more than fifty books, including the Pulitzer Prize–winning *The Children of Crisis* series and the first biography, *Erik H. Erikson: The Growth of His Work* (1970). A comprehensive biography was published in 1999 after a decade of work by Indiana University historian Lawrence Friedman. Friedman's earlier work, *Menninger: The Family and the Clinic,* is widely cited as a model of probing analysis into the culture of psychiatry and its impact on American society.

Robert Coles knew the Eriksons better than any of the other authors in this book, though several had at least a brush with these fascinating people. For Robert Coles and Jane Coles, Erik Erikson entered their lives from side-stage as they were seeking a script to explain the actions of children and adults who were struggling with the racial integration of the South. He was curious about what they were up to; they, at least initially, were doubtful of their own chances of explaining anything to anyone. As the encounter unfolds in the next chapter, we will see a memorable personality take on flesh and blood.

Erikson was neither a prophet speaking from on high nor a lab-coated scientist dissecting human experience. He was, as Coles's reminiscence reveals, an artist—imagining, sketching, painting, observing, painting over, standing back, and signing his name to one creation before moving on to another. For the Coles's, Erikson showed them not *the* way, but *a* way of getting hold of a complicated reality and of seeing it in living form. They, like Erikson himself, could, then, turn and present the picture they had composed to an audience in need of a vision. Both Erik Erikson and Robert Coles would win the Pulitzer Prize for their artistry.

For a prospective biographer, one quite accustomed to complex subjects, Erik Erikson posed a formidable challenge. After all, Erikson has his own theory about the very subject of biography—namely, identity. As Lawrence Friedman discovers, Erikson also had a life—an amazingly full and elusive kind of life. Here Friedman reveals how he tried to work with

Erikson's eight-stage theory, with Erikson's own autobiographical self-accounting in six stages, and, finally, with the shifting ground and twisting paths of Erikson's own journey.

What emerged were insights into the interchange of theory and practice. As both Erikson and Friedman notice, it was one thing to hypothesize that elements of identity came from within the "I" and quite another to be able to observe them at the source. Yet the behavior became a clue to the origins, as well as the connection to the surroundings. In Friedman's picture, we see Erikson making himself known in contexts of personal struggle with a family tragedy, in political controversies with Red-baiting politicians, and in professional encounters with defined disciplines that cast him in the role of outsider. Friedman concludes with his afterthoughts following a decade of work on Erikson and an assessment of his legacy. With that, we have a rounded conception of Erik Erikson, the theorist, and can now turn to his creation, the theory.

Developmental psychologists James Marcia of Simon Fraser University and Jane Kroger of the University of Tromsø have devoted their careers to the testing, interpretation, and extension of Erikson's concepts. Marcia created the "Identity Status Interview" and is the seminal figure in the systematic research that many scholars around the world have conducted over the last three decades. Jane Kroger's work centers on identity formation and maintenance from early stages through adulthood and, in this chapter, to maturity. Marcia and Kroger survey the research, reflect on what has been learned, and point to the frontiers of cross-cultural research in identity formation.

James Marcia tours us through thirty-five years of research based on structured interviews that probe a substantial part of the sequence of developmental challenges specified by Erikson. The patterns Erikson named appear with remarkable consistency in the findings of more than 500 studies and twice that number of dissertations. While Marcia's stream of research is not the only Eriksonian approach, it is the most widely cited and systematic. What becomes clear is that what Erikson saw in his patients, and what he pictured in his writings, were constructs that meet the test of verifiability across a wide range of subjects living in quite different contexts.

Were Marcia only a researcher synthesizing empirical studies, his insight into Erikson's legacy would not be as compelling as it is. His work as a therapist brings to life the dynamics of Erikson's theory. He makes us see how people fashion answers to life challenges out of the material around and within them. He also takes us into the world of the therapist who draws strategies and tactics from Erikson's comprehensive view of developmental strategies. What Marcia finds in his own therapeutic experience is validation for Friedman's finding after researching Erikson's clients—that Erikson was on the right therapeutic track as evidenced by the recovery rate of his patients.

James Marcia ends his essay in a reflective comment about the personal relevance of an Eriksonian perspective, and Jane Kroger, a researcher of similar interests, takes up the examination of Erikson's theory on the same note. Erikson's life can be viewed as one long seminar comprised of colleagues in several disciplines, graduate and undergraduate students, patients, and, above all, Joan Erikson. Kroger came in upon the later stages of this seminar and witnessed first-hand the interplay that was formative for Erikson's work. She brings this sense of interplay to her evocative description of identity formation and maturation.

Stepping back from the literature, Kroger places Marcia's stream of research alongside her own. She pushes on to an exploratory study of the late stages of exploration and commitment characteristic of old age. While many would see the elderly as past players in the game of life, Kroger finds them active in tasks that affirm the underlying structure of Erikson's theory. We can see the synergy of adaptation and consistency in the most successful cases of identity resolution, and we can also see the unresolved tensions in the least successful cases.

Next, the applications of concepts of identity are taken up by political scientists Kristen Monroe of the University of California—Irvine and Kenneth Hoover of Western Washington University. Monroe's study of altruists, specifically rescuers of Jews from the Nazis, have taken us to new levels of understanding human motivation. Her work establishes the primacy of identity-based motivational accounts over the alternatives, such as rational choice theory. Kenneth Hoover has written about the political implications of identity in five books and here presents a synthesis of research on identity and its meaning for democracy. The chapter points the way toward public policies that nurture healthy identities while strengthening democratic politics.

Kristen Monroe compares identity theory with another powerful paradigm: rational choice theory. The attempt to reduce human behavior to a series of calculations based on self-interest has fascinated social scientists for at least two centuries. In the last few decades, rational choice has taken over substantial parts of the disciplines of economics, political science, and sociology. Monroe, fully trained in this perspective, began to challenge it with her remarkable studies of altruists, philanthropists, heroes, rescuers, and, now, perpetrators of atrocities.

By comparing insights drawn from across the range of behavior, Kristen Monroe has charted the reach of motivations that are not accounted for by self-interest. She has turned up compelling evidence of the ways that identity constrains choice and of the vital need for connection with others that takes such powerful forms in the lives of her subjects. Her work is at the intersection of political science, moral philosophy, and psychology—a rare combination that yields some gripping narratives of human bravery and cruelty.

With these insights drawn from a variety of researches into Erikson's theory, the discussion in the next chapter turns to political action. How can identity be reconciled with democracy? After centuries of experience with monarchs, dictators, aristocracies, and revolutionary regimes, democracy has become the most prevalent, and celebrated, form of governance. The events of September 11, 2001, have forced a confrontation with a grim possibility—that democracy may not be able to accommodate the claims of identity-seeking groups willing to employ violence to achieve recognition.

While governments struggle to contain the threat of violence without abandoning constitutional freedoms, deeper questions lurk beneath the surface: What policies and processes can democracies offer that will address the inherent desire for identity? How can democracies be proactive in meeting legitimate claims to identity? By what rationale can democracies limit the excesses of chauvinism, discrimination, and repression that are tools of negative identity formation? What is there in Erikson's theory and the subsequent research that points toward solutions to these tangled questions? Some intriguing answers are to be found by building upon the empirical research reported here.

The dangers of doing nothing to strengthen the relationship of democracy and identity formation is illustrated copiously in the next two chapters. Catarina Kinnvall of Lund University and Lina Haddad Kreidie of the University of California-Irvine are of a new generation of political scientists who are deploying the analytical power of the concept of identity in addressing contemporary crises. Kinnvall takes us to sites where the shock of globalization leads people to seek a basis for their sense of self amidst the deepest crises their cultures have experienced. Kreidie, viewing the world from a Muslim perspective, opens to view the identities of people with varying kinds of commitments to Islam.

Catarina Kinnvall surveys the impact of globalization upon structures and processes of identity development. In shaping her synthesis of Erikson and several contemporary theorists, Kinnvall brings in a discussion of Marxist theories of structural change and, more extensively, the works of Vamik Volkan and Julia Kristeva. She sees the dialectical nature of Erikson's theory and its emphasis on context as a bridge between personal psychology and forces of social change. At the same time, as globalization (of which democratization is a component) proceeds, ever larger sectors of the world population find themselves on shifting grounds. The assertion of nation over state may be seen as an assertion of the self against the depersonalizing forces of a marketized economy and a democratized polity.

Turning to Volkan's studies of "chosen traumas," Kinnvall illustrates the ways that communities bereft of identity seek to recapture cohesion by invoking memories of historical affronts at the hands of others (or "glories" in the form of victories). This dynamic plays into the objectification of "the other" and the pseudospeciation that Erikson witnessed in his own work on racial and cultural discrimination. Yet Kinnvall is not satisfied with a displacement model of this sort and brings in Kristeva's Lacanian perspective to probe the relatedness of affirmation and negation in the struggle for identity. In doing so, we become aware of why identity is a lifelong process with both positive and negative valences.

Finally, Lina Kriedie brings to the discussion her interviews with Muslim believers. She pursues the comparison of identity relations and rational choice theories in understanding how Muslims construe their own worldview and their relations to those with other beliefs. Kreidie interviewed a range of believers, from the newly converted and totally committed to the more secularly oriented among the faithful. This permits her to see the interplay between identity and rational choice at differing levels of commitment.

Kreidie's work lays open the difficult question of how to moderate relations between nations when fundamentalist approaches overtake secular modernism and its avenues of compromise through diplomatic relations and trade agreements. The insights into the mindset of those whose faith is literal and all encompassing returns the inquiry to the central questions of identity and its importance to the survival of civilization.

The Future of Identity

As the world moves ever closer to a truly globalized social and economic structure, the forces that organize the cultural milieu that young (and old) people develop within will increasingly threaten received hopes and aspirations. As Jessica Stern observed recently, "Uneasiness with liberal values, discomfort with uncertain identities, and resentment of the privileged are perennial problems in modern societies. What is new today is that radical leaders are using the tools of globalization to construct new, transnational identities based on death cults, turning grievances and alienation into powerful weapons."[7]

Therein lies the real challenge for psychologists, political scientists, educators—indeed, all who influence human development: How will we be able to realize a balance between the impersonal forces of globalization and the needs of humanity. As we will see, there is room for considered approaches to identity relations that build relationships across ostensible differences—but only if the nature of identity is fully understood.

The first step in resolving any problem is to clearly understand what is at issue. Erik Erikson certainly has a cornucopia of insight and—something seldom mentioned in modern academic discourse—much *wisdom* to offer.

Notes

1. This project originated at an "Erik Erikson Centennial Symposium" at the Berlin meetings of the International Society of Political Psychology (ISPP) in 2001. We wish to acknowledge with thanks the contribution of Dana Ward, ISPP Executive Director, to the symposium. Subsequently, the participants identified those who could add the most to an assessment of "the future of identity," and the present set of chapters is the result.

2. In Anthony Giddens' *Modernity and Self-Identity* (Cambridge, England: Polity Press, 1991), intersections between contemporary sociological phenomena and the psychoanalytic dimensions of identity are explored. His work is not easily placed in any one of these schools, though his definition of identity as "the self as reflexively understood by the person in terms of her of his biography," places him closer to the perspective discussed here than to any one of the schools I have cited. Cf. p. 53.

3. While the findings incorporated here are generally accepted, the further extensions of Gilligan's work remain quite controversial. Cf. Carol Gilligan, *In a Different Voice: Psychological Theory and Women's Development* (Cambridge, Mass.: Harvard University Press, 1982); Carol Gilligan et al., *Mapping the Moral Domain: A Contribution of Women's Thinking to Psychology* (Cambridge, Mass.: Harvard University Press, 1988); Carol Gilligan et al., eds., *Making Connections: The Relational Worlds of Adolescent Girls at Emma Willard School* (Cambridge, Mass.: Harvard University Press, 1989). Eva E. Skoe and James E. Marcia, "A Measure of Care-Based Morality and Its Relation to Ego Identity," *Merrill-Palmer Quarterly* 37, 2 (April 1991): 289–304. A thorough discussion of feminist views of Erikson's works may be found in Gwendolyn Sorell and Marilyn Montgomery, "Feminist Perspectives on Erikson's Theory: Their Relevance for Contemporary Identity Development Research," *Identity: An International Journal of Theory and Research* 1, 2 (2001), http://gessler.ingentaselect.com/vl=7322155/cl=112/nw=1/rpsv/cgibin/linker?ini=erlbaum&reqidx=/catchword/erlbaum/15283488/v1n2/s1/p97 (October 1, 2003).

4. Discussed in detail in Kenneth Hoover, with James Marcia and Kristen Parris, *The Power of Identity: Politics in a New Key* (New York: Chatham House/Congressional Quarterly Press, 1997). Chapter Seven, by James Marcia, reviews the empirical research. Cf. J. E. Marcia, A. S. Waterman, D. R. Matteson, S. L. Archer, and J. L. Orlovsky, *Ego Identity: A Handbook for Research* (New York: Springer-Verlag, 1993).

5. The terms *community* and *commitment* were suggested by Donald Emmerson as more communicative than *integrality* and *mutuality*—the terms used in *The Power of Identity* and derived directly from Erikson's clinical research.

6. Erikson himself had no formal departmental affiliation at Harvard and was not able to chair doctoral committees as a result. Consequently, he had few

trained followers to amplify and extend the findings arising from his research. Those who were most deeply influenced by his teaching, among them Robert Coles and Carol Gilligan, were more likely to strike out on their own and pursue distinctive and even contrary lines of inquiry—a development Erikson supported, as Coles reports, though he sometimes regretted the results. Cf. Lawrence Friedman, *Identity's Architect: A Biography of Erik H. Erikson* (New York: Scribner, 1999), 426.

7. Jessica Stern, "The Protean Enemy," *Foreign Affairs* 82: 4, July/August 2003, http://www.foreignaffairs.org/20030701faessay15403/jessica-stern/the-protean-enemy.html (November 17, 2003).

Part One

Origins

Chapter Two

Remembering Erik

Robert Coles

In 1961 my wife, Jane, and I were living in Vinings, Georgia, then a small rural community to the northwest of fast-growing Atlanta. Each weekday, Monday through Friday, we visited one or another of the four high schools whose students, white and African American, had begun going to classes together—the onset of court-ordered desegregation. After school, we went to one or two homes, there to talk with particular youths, and their parents, about how a very tense climate of fear and suspicion was coming to bear on their lives, not to mention those of other classmates, and, too, the lives of their teachers. I was then a thirty-year-old child psychiatrist, only recently done with my training; and, quite frankly, I wasn't at all sure that what I was doing had any real use or significance for me, let alone for the young men and women whom I was getting to know as a doctor from up north who had stumbled into the South's school desegregation crisis out of an accident, rather than as part of a planned research effort.

I had entered the Air Force in 1958, under the old doctor's draft, and been sent to Biloxi, Mississippi, where for two years I worked at Keesler Air Force base as a military psychiatrist. I often went into nearby New Orleans to attend medical meetings at Tulane's School of Medicine and conferences at the New Orleans Psychoanalytic Institute. So doing, I had to make my way through that old port city's streets—and one day found such a journey to be difficult indeed. Street crowds were everywhere, some of them become riotous mobs, intent on blocking the entry of the six-year-old African-American children assigned to two elementary schools by officials complying reluctantly with a federal judge's orders, rather than approaching a crisis with sincere helpfulness. As I got to know the young people involved, and the adults who were running the schools, I began to wonder whether I was learning much of any value to anyone—I had started out as an accidental observer, then had taken pains to meet some of the children and others who were attending a troubled city's schools.

My wife and I had moved to Atlanta in an effort to learn more—to find out how desegregation worked for high schoolers who were more inclined to speak readily, and to be more immediately forthcoming to Jane and me than the first graders we'd met and come to know in New Orleans (though years later, the drawings and paintings of those young- sters would prove of lasting instructional value). In both Louisiana and Georgia, for all my experience in pediatrics, then adult and child psychia- try, I began to feel at loose ends, if not at a decided loss. My friends and colleagues of medical school and residency days, were now busy in hospi- tals, outpatient clinics, offices, developing careers for themselves, and my wife's former teaching associates were busy at work in the Boston high school where she had taught, and there we were, not only asking children how their school lives were going, but wondering what these informal, home visits were teaching us—and to what purpose in our decidedly un- conventional working lives. We had no institutional base, no office, no research design or proposal to implement, no salary, even. We were drawing on our savings, in a region we'd only begun to know and under- stand, and we had no conferences or seminars to attend (with all the per- sonal and professional support they offer).

One day Jane and I went to the Vinings post office, and thereafter back home, started sorting the mail (which the post mistress, mischie- vously once called our "Yankee letters"—as if from a distant country of some notoriety). One envelope stood out—it had Harvard University on the outside, a school Jane and I knew as one-time students. The writer identified himself as a teacher there, and explained the reason for his writing to us: he had heard through a mutual friend, a young historian also teaching at the college, that we were getting to know some of the children who had initiated school desegregation, and that we were also involved with what was soon to be known as the sit-in efforts of SNCC, the Student Non-Violent Coordinating Committee, an aspect of the civil rights struggle then spreading across the states of the Old Confederacy. The writer asked this: "Might we one day meet?" He offered a phone number, and expressed his strong interest in what was happening across Dixie—"of importance to all of us," was a phrase used: one that Jane and I would keep in mind for its quietly affirmative tone. In no time, we were back to our daily, home-visiting routines, and the letter we had received left our consciousness, which had impressions and facts aplenty to retain and try to understand.

One late afternoon, upon our return to our apartment, we heard the phone ringing, and Jane answered it. The caller identified himself as "Professor Erikson," said he taught at Harvard College, and asked whether he had the right number for Jane and me, who (he was told through a mutual friend) were "studying desegregation in Louisiana and Georgia." Yes, we were the ones, Jane said, and then an invitation: were we ever up north, and near Cambridge, Massachusetts, might we meet? Yes, Jane said, though with no great enthusiasm or conviction—nor had we any idea when such a visit would take place (the question had been asked).

Eventually, Jane and I did go north on a visit to our families, and on that occasion we did get to see Professor Erikson—we met him for a cup of coffee, took a walk with him, and even then heard him express gratitude for being able to teach and get to know college students; but we also heard him criticize much of the academic life he had, for the first time, come to witness firsthand. Memorably, he said this: "The young people teach Joan and me a lot—but there is more than enough snobbery here, I'm afraid." So much there, right off (we would later realize) that tells of Erikson—his mention of his wife, Joan, as a spokesperson as well as a companion, and his disdain for a well-known university's version of pomp and circumstance. Indeed, I recall so well the time he took me to the Harvard faculty club for lunch. We were standing in a line, waiting to be seated, and there was plenty to hear—professors talking about this or that. The language was fairly academic, and I did take silent note of it, with no great pleasure; but Erik smiled broadly—and then this: "When you folks finish your work down South, taking on arrogance, you might do some work up here, in places like this." After those words, a shrug of his shoulders, and a shake of his head—as if to emphasize physically, quite personally, what he was hearing and observing with considerable dislike.

The students, though, were a big reward for him, gave him lots to ponder, as he prepared his weekly lectures for them in his "Human Development" course, which took its participants through his well-known "life cycle," which he sometimes playfully pronounced as if it had wheels and was meant to carry willing riders. I have seen many professors at ease with students, but never quite with the eager attentiveness Erik offered them. "I learn so much from them," he once remarked—rarely a refrain to be heard in the buildings he was then frequenting for the giving of lectures, or for a meal now and then. He also followed the students elsewhere; he dined with them, took walks with them, received a steady stream of them during his office hours. Often the students came in pairs, the young men and women a youthful echo of the professor whose wife was constantly there—at his lectures or walking with him, strolling together affectionately across a campus. "I've never met or even seen any of the wives of any of my professors," one student told me—and then this: "Erikson is different." The young woman added this: "His wife is with him all the time—and when she's not there, he keeps mentioning her."

So much to that offhand observation, I would gradually realize, as I got to know Erik better. His ideas, his writing, always passed Joan's attentive, knowing muster—even as she was the one who persuaded him to leave the tight-knit Viennese psychoanalytic community which he'd inadvertently entered as a teacher of children whose parents had come from the world over to see Freud and his colleagues (including his daughter Anna, who spotted young Erik Homburger at work with schoolchildren, and suggested he study psychoanalysis with her—a big chapter in Erik's life).

There would be, of course, for Erik and Joan, other important moments, decisions, initiatives, considerations and reconsiderations. Erik was never a lock-step careerist—he was constantly surprising even himself, let alone others. I recall him, in his sixties and seventies, going back to times of decision in his life, as he tried to make sense of how he became the person he then was. In a sense, he was putting to word a particular life's gradual emergence, formation: "It's a mystery, how we become the people we become! I never went to college—I was a high school dropout, in today's language, and now I'm called a professor here. I was an artist, who stumbled into a teaching job and then into "The Freud Circle," they were called. Then I met Joan, a Canadian studying in Europe—and lo and behold, I became an American! Talk about luck—though you have to be ready, I'll admit, when luck comes and knocks on your door: ready to say yes, I'll take a chance!

"You ask me to describe myself with an adjective or two [I was then working on a *New Yorker* profile of him, and had wondered aloud how he might speak of his own life—the emergence of the 'identity' of the person who made so very much of that word—gave it so many layered meanings]. Well, I guess I'll hesitate, and end up wandering all over the map with avowals and disclaimers! But if I had to limit myself to a few words, I'd say that I was restless, maybe a bit rebellious, always one who looked and looked, then listened closely. I can tell that I'm hedging my bets here, psychologically, as we all do, so often; but let's settle for 'restless,' not as an element of psychopathology (who is without some of that!)—but as an eagerness to keep exploring (again: looking and looking). Here I'd better stop, leave it as it is, the subject of my subjectivity!"

Vintage Erikson, I then thought—his constant effort to circle around things, and thereby take their fullest, widest measure. What a tape-recorder can't document, however, is the speaker's bodily posture, facial expressions, as he has his say. Erik was circling around himself, so to speak, he was testing things with his arms, sometimes his right, sometimes his left, sometimes pointing, sometimes moving his hand up or down or sideways—an artist at work, I remember thinking, looking carefully, the upper limbs painting away, with language as the medium, in this case, of the speaker's self-expression (even as the hands were moving to convey a life's vigorous mobility).

Once, in 1964, I went with Erik and Joan to Mississippi—he was working on his Gandhi book, and he wanted to witness the nonviolent efforts of American students to challenge the bastion of segregation, some of them former members of his college class. Erik was ever wanting to see and see, then move on—so as to see more, learn more, know more: a memorable demonstration of energetic engagement with people, with a place, with so much history that was then unfolding. I remember exhaustion setting in—all of us needing a break from a hectic, demanding, and troubling day's documentary work (so much to hear and see). But Erik was unflagging, always eager to add more to the growing store of sights and sounds that had come our way, even as Joan and I suggested a pause here and there! "Yes," he turned to me once, as he looked with obvious admiration at what some young Americans had accomplished—the building of a school and clinic for needy children; and then this: "So much to witness here—history in the making, people building their future." Those words, I realized, were Erik's way of describing not only others at work, but his own life's work, his relentless insistence that childhood be understood, that a society be observed, that the deeds of those who enter history be put on the record—the why's of their personal lives become instruments of history's march forward, all told the rest of us by Erik the artist become psychoanalyst, become teacher, become writer, become biographer and historian. Such a presence, his, such a presence, Joan's, such a joint presence, theirs, many of us fondly remember, and still sorely miss!

Chapter Three

Erik Erikson:

A Biographer's Reflections

on a Decade-Long Process

Lawrence Friedman

Early in 1990 I went to New York to review final details for the spring publication of *Menninger: The Family and the Clinic* with the Knopf publishing house. Nine years in the making, it explored the interrelationship between the founding Menninger family and its historically renowned psychiatric clinic. A psychologically dysfunctional family made for a dysfunctional clinic, the argument ran. Although the study was not intended to be a biography, Karl Menninger's presence, brilliance, and erratic temperament were at the heart of the study. "Its darned near a biography," my editor insisted.

That evening I had dinner with two New York friends, writers, and fellow political activists—Robert J. Lifton and Charles Strozier. Both suggested that after Karl Menninger, I "do" their friend Erik Erikson. After all, I knew Erikson modestly and had been teaching his books for decades. Erikson's *Young Man Luther* (1958) had shown those of us who had helped to launch the "psychohistory" movement the magnificent insights that could accrue by fusing a flexible psychoanalytic psychology with daring, imaginative historical questions. I told Lifton and Strozier that I liked the idea of "doing Erik." However, I needed to check with him and his wife Joan and to determine the state of the newly deposited Erikson papers at Harvard's Houghton Library.

By spring, just after *Menninger* came out, I spent a week in Cambridge, Massachusetts. Erik and Joan Erikson lived there, roughly four blocks from the Houghton Library, where the papers had recently been deposited by theologian Dorothy Austin, their housemate/caretaker. (During "spring cleaning" Joan had placed the papers in plastic trash bags which Austin rescued at curbside as a garbage truck approached.) I spent five or six days surveying these papers—a fairly substantial collection—and realized that they were the basis for a full scale biography. After periodic teas that week with the Eriksons, the two signed consent forms that allowed me to study all Erikson material anywhere—personal, public, and clinical—without restrictions. Erik fretted to Joan that a biography would "ruin us," but Joan reassured him. The project had been launched. Now the task was to gain perspective on Erik's life and thought—a much greater difficulty than I had anticipated.

I

Soon after becoming Erik Erikson's biographer, I met with David Wilcox, a child development psychologist and the last clinician that aging Erik had supervised under special arrangements with Cambridge Hospital. One day in the late 1980s, Wilcox had brought materials to Erikson's house from a four-year-old boy with whom he had been working. He arranged various toys on the floor as the boy had arranged them and presented the child's tic tac toe grids. Erikson spent much time studying and asking questions about the items, wondering about several particulars that Wilcox had not considered significant. He told Wilcox that play, like a dream, opened the child's inner life—the unconscious. But play also told much about the child's specific social and family circumstances. Nothing could ever be left out of the clinician's consideration. "REMEMBER," Erikson emphasized, "EVERYTHING IS OUR BUSINESS." He proceeded to point out items in the child's play arrangements that were easy to ignore and explained to Wilcox how these revealed significant aspects of both the child's inner emotional life and outer social circumstances. The old man was still a brilliant and subtle clinician.

When I attended graduate school in history in the mid-1960s, "everything is our business" was basic dogma. Historians were suppose to look at every conceivable bit of evidence on their topics. But it became all too obvious that historians and other professionals honored this requirement in the breach; there was simply too much data in too many locations and too many time constraints to look at "everything." Nonetheless, old man Erikson meant what he said. Because deep insights could be derived from the most obscure part of a toy construction or a tic tac toe grid, literally everything had to be looked at. Not long after launching my biography, I realized that I literally had to approximate this goal—to try to look at Erikson with a clinician's fine eye—if I was to capture his life in much of its complexity. During all of his existence, the man constantly—sometimes hourly—shifted about in his moods, his thoughts, and his actions, and I needed to try to follow these changes through nine decades. To reduce the life and thought to set generalizations and regular patterns was to blunder badly.

Very early on, I conferred with Erikson's two prior biographers—Robert Coles (1970) and Paul Roazen (1976). Both published before the Houghton Library collection had existed. But they had rapport with a younger and more vibrant Erikson at the peak of his influence. Coles and Roazen shared materials with me. I also read the massive Erikson secondary literature—dissertations, articles, and short books in German and English. Though some of these works were deeper than others, I realized they focused on select aspects of the man's published thought and wholly missed the ever-changing complexities of the life from which those thoughts emerged.

To capture Erikson in his full, always-changing complexity, and to avoid rendering another work of reductionist scholarship, my first response was to find every existent shred of evidence about the man. The Houghton collection was heaviest after 1970, and I needed to travel to archives throughout the world that had more pieces of the Erikson story—Karlsruhe, Vienna, Copenhagen, London, San Francisco, and other locations. I also interviewed and reinterviewed prodigiously all living members of the Erikson family and most of his friends, colleagues, and enemies—well over a hundred people. I studied all available clinical case conference reports where he had participated, large numbers of his clinical records, FBI files, and even confidential faculty files at Berkeley and Harvard. Since "everything" was "my business," I struggled over the years to see all. In the course of a decade, I probably saw considerably more than earlier investigators. But in the years since 1999, when *Identity's Architect* was published, important new information from family and friends continued to surface. If it was naïve to think that I could know everything, the quest to make "everything" my preoccupation had still been a useful prod.

II

Erikson probably deserved to be called the leading exemplar of psychobiography through *Young Man Luther* (1958), which focused on the Protestant Reformation leader's late adolescent "identity crisis, " and *Gandhi's Truth* (1969), which concerned the Mahatma in midlife preoccupied with his personal and political ability to give or generate life and help to others. Adolescent identity issues and midlife generativity concerns were stops on Erikson's eight-stage model of the human life cycle, beginning with the infant's issues of trust and mistrust and ending with the elderly person's conflict between a sense that his life had integrity and a feeling of despair. A temptation, of course, was to structure my biography of Erikson along the developmental lines he had laid out for all human beings, stage by stage. An Eriksonian biography of Erikson, seemed eminently sensible. After all, was not his model of a universal life cycle congruent with his own life?

Apparently not. Between 1968 and 1975 Erikson published his three versions of an autobiographical essay, and the developmental stages he described for himself in each differed significantly from his life cycle model. For one, he plotted six and not eight stages to his life, and they focused not so much on the emotions of inner life but upon the social, occupational, and ethical concerns of his adulthood. The first five stages of his model (from the trust vs. mistrust dichotomy of infancy to the identity vs. role confusion clash at adolescence) were collapsed into the first twenty-five years of his life. He characterized the second stage of his life to be his six years in Vienna (1927–33) where he acquired "Training" and stability—his Freudian idea system, a psychoanalytic vocation, a wife who grounded him firmly in day-to-day realities, and two children. Nor did Erikson's third autobiographical stage correspond to his developmental model. It represented the years from his arrival in America in 1933 to the publication in 1950 of his first book, *Childhood and Society*. He characterized the 1950s as the third stage in his life—a period that began with his failure to find his own voice in the crisis over the McCarthyite faculty loyalty oath at the University of California, witnessed his efforts to help adolescent patients discover their voices at the Austen Riggs Center, and culminated with his second book in which he described how Luther discovered his full voice and identity. Erikson considered the 1950 to 1975 interval as his fifth stage—his period as a renowned Harvard professor and ethical philosopher. Old age stood for the last years of his life and his entry into "the shadow of nonbeing."

Because these six autobiographical stages drew upon and interpreted what Erikson saw to be the broad directions of his own existence, I gave them more credence as biographer than his formal model of the life cycle. Indeed, they were easier to document with written contemporary evidence than fragments and speculations on his early years. However, I was mindful that Erikson had written about Gandhi's autobiography three years before he published the first essay on his own life that "autobiographies are written at certain stages of life for the purpose of recreating oneself in the image of one's own method; and they are written so as to make that image convincing." Five single-spaced pages of notes on the major and minor variations in Erikson's three published versions of his autobiography suggested the importance with which he regarded his effort to present himself to the world as he entered late life. Moreover, although his autobiography emphasized his outer social and intellectual life, I was unwilling to belittle Erikson's inner emotions, especially during his early years and adolescence.

At base, my biography was Eriksonian in the sense that, like his own biographical studies, I was deeply attentive to the intersection of his inner emotions and his outer social circumstances. But I found his universal eight-stage life cycle largely inapplicable to the data I uncovered concerning his own existence and his six-stage autobiography only a somewhat more helpful guide. In the end, I simply allowed the fundamental issues in the course of his life to unravel and analyzed the continuities and breaks of a life in process. "Context is everything," he frequently emphasized, and I allowed the twists and turns of his emotions, thoughts, actions, and contexts to shape the Erikson story.

III

My preliminary title for the biography was *Border Crossings: A Life of Erik H. Erikson*. The more I learned about the man, the more uncomfortable I became with standard descriptive labels. Yes, he was a psychoanalyst but also an ethicist and an artist. He thought with an acute and logical mind, but he also thought visually in pictures and diagrams. At times he rambled and was nearly incoherent. He considered himself a Dane, but sometimes also a German and increasingly after 1933 an American. Asked whether he was a Jew or a Christian, he characteristically replied, "Why both, of course." Even on that matter, his emphasis regularly shifted. Sometimes he regarded himself as a mentor, at times as a student, periodically a guru, sometimes a teacher and writer, and sometimes simply a loner. In his clinical and scholarly work, he sometimes followed Freud and focused vertically into the inner life of the self. But at other times he focused horizontally on the society and milieu around the inner self. Most often, as in his analysis of Freud's work on the famous Irma dream, he saw the manifest or outer form of the dream as coequal in importance with the deep inner or latent dream content.

The perspective of Erikson as a constant border crosser who was always in process and very difficult to pin down surfaced again and again in the course of my investigations. In 1965 he spoke at Harvard at the memorial service for theologian Paul Tillich, his friend and colleague. The theme was that Tillich too had been a border crosser—constantly walking over traditional lines of demarcation. Like himself, Tillich had been a German but also an American and liked to live on the edges of the United States (west and east coast). He, like Tillich, shifted constantly in his vocational identities. Both had ties to an amorphous sort of Protestantism the tenets of which modified constantly. After the memorial service, Erikson walked through Cambridge for hours with his graduate student, Richard Hunt, and recounted that, like Tillich, he had enjoyed crossing borders and avoiding fixed positions or identifying characteristics. Life consisted of shifts back and forth across multiple edges. Even in old age, he preferred the borders. When I visited Erikson in May of 1992, for example, I brought Hetty Zock's closely textured new book, *A Psychology of Ultimate Concern*, which traced the interplay between his deepening existentialist and spiritualist orientations. Erikson objected to "ultimate concern" as too rigid and deterministic a characterization. A lot more had been on his mind, and matters of "ultimate concern" represented but one of the threads or trajectories. In mid-January of 1994, a few months before his death and an interval when he could mumble but not speak, I visited Erikson in his room at a nursing home in Harwich, Massachusetts. Even as the end approached, his eyes shifted about constantly (a sort of cognitive crossing) from the Danish flag on his chest of drawers to a box of chocolates on a ledge to his name on the door to the scenery outside his window. He smiled and frowned and laughed and pondered and dozed. Never before had I seen a very elderly, disabled person in such variable states.

If even in his last months, Erikson was so variable and changing, it was difficult to summarize the essence of most of his written texts. *Childhood and Society* (1950), for example, represented at least a dozen years of formulating and reformulation of his thoughts about Hitler's appeal to German youth, the nature of dreams, the culture of the Sioux and the Yurok, his most compelling clinical experiences, Gorky's childhood within central Russia, and the centrality of identity to the eight-stage life cycle. Even after the book came out, he penciled in thematic and literary modifications. The second edition of *Childhood and Society* in 1963 was a very different book, in many respects, than the first, but even that underwent extensive post-publication penciled modifications. Erikson's last significant publication, "The Galilean Sayings and the Sense of 'I'" (*Yale Review*, April 1981), was eight years in the making. It was sparked by his sense that there was something deeper than his concept of human identity – that humankind was connected by the sense of "I." To understand the nature of this "I," Erikson had initially turned to Jefferson's compilation of Jesus' "authentic" sayings. In 1973, he had given a lecture sponsored by the National Endowment for the Humanities on the protean third President and what Jesus' sayings revealed to Jefferson about the essential nature of the conscious self. Next Erikson considered writing a biography of Kierkegaard to understand the "I"—the full conscious self at its most profound level—but found that his Danish was insufficient. Finally, he settled on pondering the nature of Jesus' Galilean ministry. At Galilea, Erikson concluded, Jesus discovered a sense of "I" at its deepest level. It was something like the Quaker Inner Light where God permeated all of humanity, connecting the individual self to all selves. Finally, as his son Kai worked with him to make the *Yale Review* essay coherent, Erikson felt compelled to explore how the "I" that one experienced in late life recreated the numinous "I" of the newborn—whether the life cycle folded back into itself. Whether it was the "Galilean Sayings" article, *Childhood and Society*, or anything else that Erikson wrote, I found that his thought and feeling underwent constant shifts as he drafted and redrafted his texts. As biographer, I felt that I could not simply summarize the final publication but had to trace the constantly shifting contemplations and life experiences as he wrote and rewrote.

IV

Because it was so difficult to write a biography of an avid border crosser who, until death, was in constant motion, especially in his thoughts and feelings, I needed somehow to ground his life—to reach a concrete human dimension. Friends and colleagues who looked at my first draft of the manuscript warned about the obvious—that they needed the particulars of Erikson's day-to-day life—what he liked to eat, his hobbies, his music preferences, even his attire. Readers needed to know a good deal more about the living human being. Initially, I simply jotted down specific details from visiting with Erik and Joan Erikson as I researched the biography. I remembered Erik's extreme dependence on Joan for day-to-day life necessities—what to wear, what he could and could not eat, and how to be sociable, for example. I observed him doze off in his chair and his genuine childlike glee when I "smuggled" a candy bar past Joan's eyes for him to devour. When my wife and I brought over a vegetarian lasagna for dinner with the Eriksons one day, I recalled that Erik consumed three sizable helpings and then, in European style, kissed my wife's hand. Generally, however, I had been so preoccupied by Erik's brilliant mind and evolving thoughts during the dozens of times I met with him that I was only able to come up with a short list of specifics on the rest of the person.

Fortunately, Erikson's youngest son, Jon, had been more attentive to the particulars. Jon provided a vast array of specifics—how his father's idea of good food was a frozen Swanson TV dinner and chocolate covered coffee beans despite his wife's attentiveness to healthful living. There were also the late-night raids on the ice cream in the freezer as Joan slept. Jon recalled that Erikson had played the piano during the 1930s and with considerable joy, and how he swam with a breast stroke to avoid wetting his hair. Jon also described how Erik was quite style conscious about his clothing. During the 1960s and early 1970s he cut quite a figure with his sweeping white hair, aviator glasses, white shoes, southwest bow tie, and blue blazer.

A wonderful photographer, Jon Erikson also urged me to be attentive to photographs of his father, supplied me a good many, and sent me to others in the family for more. For the first time I noticed his stark blue eyes, the situations where he had been stiff and uncomfortable, and where he had been more relaxed and joyous. I could see his unhappiness as a young child and especially as an adolescent in Karlsruhe. I noted how he manifested a more grounded and contented existence when, at twenty-five, he moved to Vienna, found a vocation (a psychoanalyst), and married a very understanding lifelong partner—Joan. Soon it became apparent that the hundreds of photographs I was looking at revealed a vast amount of important detail on the man. The exercise prompted me to go further—to review the woodcuts Erik made as a young man, his doodles, and sketches of patients and acquaintances, and the multi-colored lines, circles, and arrows amidst words and phrases that repre-sented "notes" for his public presentations. After a few years of reviewing all the visual materials I could find, it struck me that Erik had never really put behind the preoccupations of his adolescence trying to succeed as an artist. He thought in shapes, shades, and colors. As I turned back to his written texts, I found that I could now see images in phrases, sen-tences, and paragraphs that I had not been able to access earlier—a Sioux medicine woman, Luther during his "fit in the choir," Gorky as a child, and even Gandhi in 1918 as he discovered the essence of nonviolent resis-tance.

If I had learned to see considerably more through Erikson's eyes, I decided to pursue the auditory more than I had. As I met with him, I tried to hear the variety of his tones and exclamations and even his si-lences, played back my tape recordings of our conversations, and made notes on the feelings that the vocal tones seemed to convey. I also lis-tened to other recordings of Erikson's voice as early as I could find them and worked on matching photographs and other visual materials with the voice at particular times. Especially through the frequent indistinctive-ness and blurring of his voice, I realized that this was a man who saw be-fore he heard (though I wish I could have heard a recording of him at the piano in the 1930s). In brief, by the end of my second draft of the biogra-phy, Erikson was becoming a fuller, more earthbound person—one who ate, slept, walked, saw, and spoke.

V

Failures in the biographical endeavor must be recounted as well as the successes. Chapter organization often tended to "freeze" or reduce a man in constant mental and even physical motion. I wrote a chapter on Erikson's migration from Europe to America during the dangerous 1930s too much along the lines of the traditional saga of the intellectual émigrés of the period. This obscured the fact that Erikson was always shifting his residence—seven times, for example, during his six years in Vienna. I devoted two chapters to *Childhood and Society*—one to his treatment of a vast array of cultures (German, American, Russian, Sioux, Yurok, etc.) and a second to his clinical presentations and the creation of his eight-stage life cycle model. In fact, he was thinking and writing about all of these topics at the same time and in terms of each other. For purposes of apparent clarity, I had "invented" two books rather than the one that he prepared. I repeated this pattern for his life and thought during the peak of his influence—the 1960s. To avoid what I feared would be an unwieldy mass, I devoted one chapter to his teaching and writing during that decade and a second chapter to his travels to India as he prepared *Gandhi's Truth* (1969). But he brought the India project to the classroom and to his other writings, and they in turn decidedly impacted the Gandhi study. For the sake of seemingly greater clarity, I was simplifying the man.

Kathleen Jones wrote a very penetrating review of *Identity's Architect* for the December 2000 *American Historical Review*. She noted that although I treated both Erikson's life and his times, the overwhelming focus was on the life. Jones was absolutely right. I found the complexity of the life so overwhelming that I did far too little on the wider context and how he impacted it—the Karlsruhe of Erikson's youth, Freud's Vienna when he was trained during the last years of the "red decade" of Social Democrat programmatic innovation, New Deal America when he became a U.S. citizen in the late 1930s, the Civil Rights and anti-Vietnam War movements of the 1960s and early 1970s as he became an icon for protest culture, and so forth. My public justification for focusing on the life over the wider context was that I had vast primary documentation on the life and needed to draw largely on the works of others for the wider world around that life (i.e., it was best to play to my strength). Retrospectively, I wonder whether that justification was actually a rationalization. For the purposes of completing the book and meeting my Scribner contractual deadline, had I slighted Erikson's admonition that "context is everything?"

A third reservation is that I may have taken too much literary license. For the past several decades, I have come increasingly to feel that good biography is a literary art and that a measure of one's success is whether one's manuscript reaches out beyond academia to the many who like a flowing, felicitous, exciting read. At least four rewrites of every chapter was required to take me to the point where I felt I had reached that goal. Was I taking too much literary license in the process, making sure that the narrative line was strong and forceful and animating, but sometimes coasting over rather dull, flat, and mundane descriptive material in the process?

This links to another issue that I still question—whether I balanced close personal empathy and sympathetic understanding of Erikson against the need for hard-nosed critical distance. I had no desire to exalt him and·had no compunctions about revealing how he and Joan had hidden a deep family secret – the birth and two-decade concealment of their fourth child, Neil Erikson, who had been badly deformed and mentally retarded owing to Down Syndrome. Erik and Joan saw him as the opposite to what normal development might be. In brief, Neil's birth represented a family crisis from which Erik and Joan worked out the concept of an eight-stage human life cycle that pivoted around fifth stage identity. Therefore the event simply had to be brought to light even as I recognized that it would "feed" the scandal mongers. In a similar vein, I felt the need to emphasize that if Erikson did not sign the McCarthy era loyalty oath as a faculty member at the University of California, he almost certainly signed a "new form of contract" that contained the language of the oath. His courage during this event was limited.

Throughout the biography, as well, I had no compunctions about underscoring his frequent vagaries and even his contradictions as a writer and theorist. Nor did I hold back on his decided shortcomings as a husband and a father. On the other hand, I felt a very close bond with the man, identifying with his reclusive life as a writer and his mixed feelings about being a public intellectual. When I jogged every morning, I thought about him. At parties and dinners, I usually made him a topic of conversation. I probably bored my students to death with Erikson stories. If I found religious experience less compelling than Erikson but political activism in progressive causes more satisfying, I regarded these as comparatively minor points of difference. We both loved the life of the mind and the writing process, and whenever I read or reread angry attacks on him by social critics whom I respected, I sometimes felt that I was being chastised.

In *Writing Lives* (1959), the brilliant Henry James biographer Leon Edel warned (p.29) that "The problem of identification is in reality at the core of modern biography, and it explains some of its most serious failures." Edel warned that "An empathetic feeling need not involve identification." Had I gone beyond deep empathy and strongly identified with the architect of identity, thereby reducing my capacity for hard-nosed criticism? Edel has given me cause to wonder.

VI

I finished my biography in the late 1990s so exhausted that I was determined never to write another. Indeed, I launched a study of those intellectual émigrés from the Holocaust who wrote psychologically penetrating studies of the rise of European fascism and authoritarianism. Within a few years, however, I found myself focusing on Erich Fromm, one of the most interesting of the lot and now, ·with sociologist Neil McLaughlin, have embarked on another full-scale biography. Moreover, I have created a senior seminar on individual lives in history and seem to have evolved into a lifetime biographer. To get at the sources of this phenomenon, I have come to the conclusion that although all proficient biographers have to be historians of social, cultural, and economic processes, the biographer's task is nonetheless distinguishable in important ways.

For one, after comparing my own experience with quite a few other historian-biographers, I have concluded that the conscientious biography can often take a good deal longer and may, in many respects, be more frustrating. The historian can skip the seemingly small details of her/his cast of characters—favorite foods, musical and sports tastes, fondness for alcohol, and mundane daily routines, for example. The biographer needs to be attentive to all of these, for all are obviously parts of the fabric of a total human life and can be quite revealing. But a biographer can hardly emulate the seventeenth-century New England Puritan minister who tried to tell all—every detail about a person or event—because all are pertinent in detecting the will of God. Consequently, after years of research on one's subject, what particulars does the biographer delete in her/his narrative? It is almost always those details that seem extraneous to her/his interpretive framework. But what if the framework is somehow flawed or reductionist or otherwise problematic as the biographer increasingly finds a stake in it through years of arduous writing and living with his subject? And can a human life, with all of its variables, coexist with even the most nuanced interpretive framework? My own sense is that this elementary dilemma becomes a conscious or semiconscious apprehension of so few biographers. It helps to explain the discomfort many of us feel when it comes time to turn our "final drafts" over to our publishing houses.

The biographer often realizes that if she/he has a lively, artfully constructed story line, all sorts of readers outside one's historic specialty area will be interested. Bookstores will stock the biography and some will ask for author presentations and book signings. National newspapers like the *New York Times* may review it and reporters may call for stories. There may be radio and television talk show appearances, formal book tours, and a piece in the *New York Review of Books* and *TLS*. Additionally, all sorts of people will write letters to the author, especially those who had contacts with the subject. Of course, academic historians are not trained for this sort of exposure We blunder about with our scholarly qualifications and hesitancies. We wonder whether we should repeat what we already said in hardcovers. We become impatient with interviewers or news people or radio call-in listeners who want clear "yes" and "no" answers. But in time, I think, we become more relaxed and even pleased by the sense that literate and curious Borders or Barnes & Noble readers and book show listeners are sharing and enjoying our pursuit of our elusive subjects. Indeed, I become a lot more respectful of people who enjoy an animating story line. A number of people in this general audience offered more penetrating observations than reviewers in academic specialty journals. As I became more open and respectful of this general audience, I found that my rapport with my own undergraduate students became more respectful and enjoyable. They had much to say that was cogent if only I would really listen to them.

Certainly, the historian of broad social or cultural processes can gain a good deal of self-understanding. But through the flow of emotions and empathies that years with one's subject inevitably provoke, the self-awareness acquired by the biographer has to be a good deal more intense. It certainly was in my case. As I learned of Joan and Erik Erikson's tragic experience of giving birth to a Down Syndrome child in an era when they were hidden in distant institutions, I thought about several of the tragedies in my own life. Indeed, while I investigated the birth of Neil Erikson, a person very close to me was on the border between life and death. As I learned how Joan and Erik Erikson blundered and even sometimes turned on one another, but eventually summoned the wherewithal to move on in their lives, I gained hope and resilience and perhaps a survivor instinct. They moved on by developing the eight-stage model of the life cycle and I moved on by finishing *Identity's Architect* and intensifying my then-flagging commitments to political activism.

Most of my firsthand experience with Erik was in his final years. I saw him experience his own late-life (eighth developmental stage) tension between thinking back on his life with a sense of integrity and pride, and reviewing his life course with gloom and despair. I devoted an entire chapter to his last years, which troubled several of my reviewers. Retrospectively, I realize that it was because I myself was crossing the divide between the generative productivities of middle age and the questions and doubts of old age. Through preoccupation with Erikson, I was drawing insight into the inevitable frailties and limitations that would occupy my own life in the years ahead and ways of dealing with them. More than ever before, I asked myself quite a few questions about how I wanted to spend my emerging old age. In sum, I cannot help but think that the biographer's experience is often an eminently introspective, indeed, therapeutic one.

Perhaps because biography has such a decided personal impact upon both the biographer and the reader, the very process of publication seems to provoke new evidence. After readers peruse a biography, some will come up with new memories and seek out additional documents. Indeed, all three of Erikson's living children flooded me with recollections that they had not offered during years of interviews. They continue to do so. Indeed, his daughter Sue Bloland launched and is about to complete a full-scale memoir and meditation on her parents. Erikson spent many anguished years trying to discover who had fathered him. Although I may have narrowed down his paternity to some Copenhagen photographers, I was far from certain. Married into the Abrahamsen Copenhagen family on his mother Karla's side, Martha Abrahamsen wrote to me a few months after publication concerning her recent conversation in Israel with one of Karla's grandchildren. Apparently, she had told the grandchild that she had many lovers during her long life but had never asked for payment from any of them. In other words, she herself may not have known who had fathered Erik. In *Childhood and Society*, Erikson wrote that he had "nothing to offer but a way of looking at things." Steven Schlein took the phrase "a way of looking at things" and made it into the title of his rich collection of many of Erikson's writings. Yet after reading *Identity's Architect*, a London psychoanalyst showed me how the phrase originated in a letter that Erikson's analyst, Anna Freud, had written in 1934 to Ernest Jones about Wulf Sachs, a member of the British Psychoanalytic Society. I could go on at length with other information—sometimes exceedingly important—that came my way subsequent to publication. I had gotten post-publication feedback with most of the books on broader historical topics that I had written, but nowhere as extensive and as crucial as the Erikson biography provoked—and continues to yield. Thus, the process of being the biographer has, in important ways, continued several years after completing the biography.

VII

When Erikson died in 1994, not a few obituaries, memorial conferences, and essays evaluated his legacy. I attended the funeral and several of the memorial conferences and read the obituaries. But I did not yet have a full measure of the man and found myself unwilling or incapable of speaking about the legacy. Four years later, realizing that *Identity's Architect* would soon be sent to my publishing house, I knew that I would have to address the legacy in the text. Perhaps because I was still so deeply immersed in Erikson's day-to-day life and thought, I wrote too vaguely and awkwardly about the legacy. But let me make a stab.

For one, the formulator of the "identity crisis" and other issues concerning identity had no fixed professional identity. He was not a psychologist, flunking his one academic psychology course, and always feeling very distant from that profession. He favored what he called "disciplined subjectivity," while the positivism and scientific claims of professional psychology troubled him. Never in his life did he even contemplate conducting empirical research. When required to state his formal discipline, Erikson tended to invoke the label "psychoanalyst." He had been trained by Freud's daughter and colleagues in Vienna to master a relatively orthodox set of doctrines and techniques and had been admitted to full membership in the Vienna Psychoanalytic Society. More-over, most of his life, he had belonged to psychoanalytic professional or-ganizations and held the highest office in one of them. But whereas Freud and his followers focused vertically, excavating the deepest inner layers of the individual human psyche, Erikson saw the necessity of linking this vertical to the horizontal–to the society and culture that surrounded the individual. One dimension was hardly less important than the other. Unlike Erich Fromm or Karen Horney, he never broke explicitly with Freud's structural theory or from the centrality of libidinal drives. But he had no patience with shoring up the structure of psychoanalytic ortho-doxy.

Was Erikson a psychohistorian? *Young Man Luther* (1958) is usually conceived of as the book that started the psychohistory movement as a subspecialty among academic historians–merging psychoanalytic under-standing with historical context. But Erikson shunned the role of "foun-der" and was distressed when several professed "psychohistorians" treated public statements of prominent historic figures like Woodrow Wilson and Georges Clemenceau as if they had originated in private therapeutic encounters. Indeed, his Luther book began as a study of his adolescent patients at the Austen Riggs Center (with an essay on adoles-cent Luther as his epilogue), but it evolved into a clinician's reflections on Luther's younger years. By the mid-1970s, after avoiding most psychohis-torical journals and practically all gatherings held in his honor, he pri-vately wished the term would have fallen into disuse.

Clearly, Erikson had no firm sense of identification with any profes-sion as such. His legacy was not a professional one. As I searched for a title for my biography, my longtime friend and colleague, Ronald Takaki, recommended *Erikson's Extravagance*. What Takaki meant was that Erikson was no austere Ahab who repressed joy and the senses in com-pulsive and austere pursuit of Moby Dick. Instead, Erikson felt that learning and thinking and doing ought to be play-like, pleasure packed, delightful, and zestful. Seeing, hearing, walking, touching, tasting, and doing–in work, lovemaking, and all else–needed to have a certain pleas-urable flare. Adults needed to discover the child in themselves–to be-come extravagantly playful–if they were to recover or sustain life's joys.

This is not to suggest that Erikson believed in the American ethic of self-help individualism–the "American Adam" or the Horatio Alger hero who, by self-exertion and a bit of luck, went on to crown his life with ma-terial success. Notions of free unfettered individuality always troubled him, particularly when they were coupled with aggrandizing materialism. Perhaps exhibiting more a European than an American sense of "iden-tity," Erikson felt that it was impossible without a connectedness to oth-ers and to one's community. The self could hardly flourish without the other. Like other ego psychologists of his generation, he maintained that optimal selfhood required some adjustment to society's customs and expectations. For this reason, several critics of the 1960s and 1970s castigated him as an architect of adjustment who was uneasy with social rebellion against injustice. In the years when that accusation gained currency, Erikson had become increasingly taken by the revolutionary leader who worked to disrupt encrusted patterns of elite domination and social conformity–to promote radical new opportunities for the society around him and for humankind. Beginning with his portrayal of young Luther launching the Reformation, then middle-aged Gandhi cultivating *Satyagraha* to garner Indian independence, next Jefferson as leader of a revolutionary new nation, and finally Jesus at Galilea discovering the "I" in human consciousness, Erikson's examples of firm ego identity were rebels who connected constructively with the Other in themselves and the others in their societies to promote radical new opportunities for humankind.

Part of Erikson's legacy belongs among mid-twentieth-century interdisciplinary Western public intellectuals who had been conditioned by the tragedies of Nazism, Stalinism, and McCarthyism, and embraced a universalist and cosmopolitan "Family of Man" perspective. Despite the contrived differences of race and ethnicity ("pseudospeciation" Erikson called it), all human beings were made of the same essential qualities and needed to be accorded the same basic dignities ("universal specieshood"). But unlike many of the cosmopolitan public intellectuals of his generation, Erikson insisted that people had to recognize the Other in themselves through a multicultural perspective. Erikson embraced the rich distinctiveness of Native Americans, Germans, Russians, Nigerians, and others. He also insisted that women were gendered creatures whose unique "inner space" fostered linkage or connectedness between humankind. In this sense, he was a forerunner of the focus since the 1960s in intellectual circles on the primacy of race, ethnicity, and gender.

As I pursued Erikson's intellectual legacy, I discovered that quite a few of his friendships among public intellectuals came not through the exchange of ideas but through his successful efforts as a therapist. He treated other intellectuals or members of their families, and this fostered lifelong friendships. David Riesman and Reinhold Niebuhr were prime examples. I reviewed the preponderance of Erikson's case files and found that most of his patients improved. He had a remarkable capacity to understand the crisis and confusion of those he treated. In case conferences, training sessions, and public presentations, Erikson explained to clinicians that the therapist had to be attentive not only to the patient's pathologies and deficiencies, but to the patient's strengths. Often it was more efficacious to build on what a patient did right than to search for underlying pathologies. He also preached against what he called the "originology fallacy"—that early experience determined subsequent psychological development. Not infrequently, it was more helpful to understand and reform the patient's current social and emotional world. Most important, Erikson built his clinical legacy on the premise that the therapist-patient connection was essentially a relationship through which both parties gained by giving to the other. Successful therapy rested heavily upon practicing the Golden Rule–possibly no more and certainly no less.

Erikson spoke to and lived the possibilities of border crossing–the excitement and freedom of shifting ideas, moods, vocations, religious proclivities, geographic settings, and more. He was a Freudian in one moment or in one paragraph, a cultural anthropologist in another, and an existentialist in another. As such, his life and work may have anticipated current discussions of the decentered sense of being that we have come to equate with postmodernism. Writing in the 1990s, his friend Robert Lifton had described the phenomenon optimistically as proteanism–a fluid and many-sided buoyancy responsive to the restless flux of the late twentieth century. Less positively, psychologist Kenneth Gergen has referred to "the vertigo of unlimited multiplicity" while psychologist Philip Cushman has described an unbounded and undifferentiated emotional hunger. However we assess the postmodern condition, Erikson's life and writings offer material for an instructive prologue.

Five years after Erikson died, two adolescents went on a killing rampage at Columbine High School in Littleton, Colorado. They belonged to a group called the Trenchcoat Mafia and thrived on Nazi weaponry, uniforms, the German language, *Mein Kampf*, celebration of Hitler's birthday, and similar particulars. Although from prosperous suburban households and outwardly concerned parents, the two killers felt deep inner senses of emptiness and inadequacy in their lives. In the wake of the national shock over Columbine, Gordon Harper and several other clinicians Erikson had trained were called upon by the *New York Times* and other media to offer expert commentary. They had no difficulty doing so. They simply cited Erikson's essay in *Childhood and Society* on Hitler's appeal to unsteady German youth. Promoting himself as the head of a juvenile delinquent gang, Hitler told German youngsters (who were not unlike the Columbine killers) to bypass their parents and local community standards of respectability and to gain identity negatively–by assaulting Jews, homosexuals, gypsies, the handicapped, Communists, and other "undesirables." One learned what one was and gained a sense of place and destiny by turning with Hitler against these enemies of the *volk*. Clinicians trained by Erikson had no difficulty pointing to resemblances between Littleton's Trenchcoat Mafia and Nazi youth gangs. Resisting the national call for greater security devices and policing of public schools, they underscored how there were no quick fixes to distraught, violence-prone adolescents. Parents and others in local communities needed to encourage inner trust, groundedness, and playfulness in children of all ages. They had to cultivate traditions of what Erikson called intergenerational reciprocity where youth and adults got and received from one another in secure, trusting environments guided by the Golden Rule. There were no shortcuts to effective if time-consuming parenting and mentoring unless one wanted to run the risks of more Columbines. Clearly, an important part of Erikson's legacy is that it is eminently usable to us as parents, grandparents, and public citizens.

Part Two

Testing, Learning, Innovating

Chapter Four

Why Erikson?

James Marcia

What does one expect of a theory? I suppose that depends upon who one is and for what purposes one needs a theory. George Kelly (1955), a psychologist forerunner unaware of postmodernism, would say that all of us construct theories in order to understand ourselves and others, and that the theories that psychologists use are distinguished primarily by their specificity and amenability to invalidation. Still, even psychologists differ in their purposes. Theories of personality development are only minimally useful to psychologists interested in memory; likewise, theories of neurological functioning are rather remote from concerns of many psychotherapists. So, in order to answer for myself the question: Why Erikson?, I must situate myself according to my interests, concerns, and purposes.

Although their relative emphasis has shifted back and forth over the past thirty-five or so years, the central areas of interest to me have been research, psychotherapy, and teaching. Some would say that that makes my interest in Erikson's theory rather peculiar, because he addresses none of these topics directly. There is no Eriksonian "school" of psychotherapy; he had a general disdain (and limited aptitude) for experimental work; and his is only one of a large number of candidates for topics in teaching courses in personality theory. Why, then, have I found his theory so compelling in all aspects of my professional life, and in many aspects of my personal life? I shall attempt to answer that question here, primarily with reference to the theory itself and my conscious motivations.

My affection for, and subscription to, Erikson's theory certainly did not arise out of personal contact. We never met. Moreover, my colleagues informed me that he was indifferent, at best, and negative, at worst, about the empirical approach that we had taken to his concept of identity.[1] He thought that such an approach might trivialize his concept. Although we were not acquainted personally with each other, Erikson's writings alone were enough for me to build a scientific career upon, to inform my therapeutic work, and to "enlighten" students.

At age twenty-four, and a young twenty-four at that, I left the graduate program in clinical psychology at Ohio State to go on my internship at Massachusetts Mental Health Center in Boston, a training hospital for Harvard Medical School. Anyone having grown up and gone to school in the Midwest will understand what an eye- and mind-widening experience this was. One of my supervisors at MMHC was David Gutmann, who had been Erikson's Teaching Assistant at Harvard. I was assigned to do a psychodiagnostic workup on a sixteen-year-old boy who was a new admission to the hospital. On both the Rorschach and TAT tests his responses indicated a fairly severe thought disorder, and we wrote up the report accordingly. The youth was subsequently released from the hospital within six months—not something one would expect from a person with a schizophrenic diagnosis. When David and I revisited our testing, he suggested that I read something. It was Erikson's *Identity and the Life Cycle* (1959). Diagnostically, our young patient was likely in a severe identity crisis which the treatment staff had helped him to pull through fairly quickly. This first contact with Erikson's theory influenced my resolution of two other problems facing me at that time.

The first was my difficulty in applying the sometimes opaque psychoanalytic jargon to my experience of my patients. With some difficulty, I was able to go through several translation phases, and finally arrive at a conceptual-experiential fit, but it was a chore. The second issue facing me upon my return from my internship to graduate work at Ohio State was the necessity of finding a dissertation topic that was worth all of the effort I knew I would put into it. Erikson's monograph, or at least what I made of it, solved both of these problems. I found a comprehensible language, sometimes even a poetic one, that bridged formal psychoanalytic theory (à la Fenichel) and what my patients were telling me, without violating their complexity or the central tenets of classical theory. In addition, I found a research topic worthy of a lifetime: the construct validation of Erikson's psychosocial developmental theory. I certainly had nothing as grand as the latter in mind when I began investigating ego identity. I knew only that it was a compelling topic, and, that if my empirically committed professors at Ohio State were right, I could tackle such an apparently unmeasurable concept using the method of construct validity.

Research

Following a number of false starts, much valuable criticism, and many suggestions from peers and professors (tinged with amused skepticism), I developed a semistructured interview and scoring manual to assess

Erikson's construct of Identity. This took the form of four styles, called statuses, of identity resolution. All four of these had been suggested, although not in such a specific manner, by Erikson's writings, as had their defining criteria: exploration (crisis) and commitment. As well, the life areas in which they were initially assessed, occupation and ideology, were drawn directly from his writings. While the criteria of exploration and commitment have remained the same over the past thirty-five years, the domains in which they are investigated have expanded to include individual's ideas about relationships, sexual orientation, ethnicity, and other topics salient to particular persons in particular contexts.

The four identity statuses are: Identity Achievement, Moratorium, Foreclosure, and Identity Diffusion. Identity Achievements have explored alternatives in key life areas such as occupation, ideology, and interpersonal values and they are committed actively to self-chosen directions in these domains They are relatively introspective, do not change their evaluations of themselves very easily under external pressures, and are on their way to establishing solidly intimate relationships. Moratoriums are right in the middle of an identity crisis, they are exploring alternatives and their commitments are usually vague, although they can be very passionate about certain social issues. They give the impression of struggling to find life directions and consequently appear as anxious. As well, their reasoning about moral issues, whether in terms of justice (Kohlberg, 1976) or care (Gilligan, 1982; Skoe and Marcia, 1991) is especially acute. Foreclosures are committed in important life areas, but these commitments are those which they have adopted from childhood authority figures. One might say that their identities are *conferred* upon them, and willingly *received,* rather than being self-*constructed* as is the case with Identity Achievements. They endorse authoritarian values and are extremely close to their families. Identity Diffusions have neither explored alternatives, nor are they committed to any particular directions in their lives. They are limited in their capacity for intimate relationships and tend to bend, ideologically, whichever way current social winds are blowing.

The identity statuses, and consequently Erikson's theory, now appear in almost all textbooks covering adolescent development. One of my goals in doing identity research during the first fifteen years of my career, besides making a reasonable living in academia, was a political one: to make Erikson sufficiently scientifically "respectable" that he would have to be included in university textbooks focusing on empirical studies. Why should I want to do that? Because his theory seemed to me, in contrast with other theories, comprehensive, comprehendible yet sophisticated, empirically translatable, and realistic in its outlook for human potential. But more on this later. The identity statuses, besides furnishing a way of understanding adolescent development, have been a point of entry for many students into Eriksonian theory, and I am pleased about that.

After the construction and validation of the identity statuses, empirical methods were applied to investigations of other measures of Eriksonian stages, broadening the empirical challenge. I shall speak here primarily of research that has been done by my students and colleagues.[2] In 1973, Jay Orlofsky and colleagues (Orlofsky, Marcia, and Lesser) developed and validated a measure of Eriksonian Intimacy/Isolation, the stage following Identity. Again, a status approach using a semi-structured interview and scoring manual was employed. Criteria were drawn from Erikson's writings about the Intimacy vs. Isolation crisis in ego growth and they included depth and commitment in relationships with a friend or romantic partner. Five Intimacy statuses were defined. Those who were classified as Intimate were engaged in committed relationships that were deep and fairly long lasting. Pre-intimated persons were similar to Intimate ones except that they were not in an enduring love relationship. Pseudo-intimate individuals were in a fairly committed romantic relationship but this relationship was fairly shallow. It had the appearance, but not the substance, of a truly intimate relationship. Persons called Stereotyped had superficial and conventional "dating" relationships. Isolate individuals withdrew from social situations and lacked any close personal relationships with peers. Some of the research providing validational evidence for these statuses is found in a handbook co-written by Marcia, Waterman, Matteson, Archer, and Orlofsky (1993).

The next Eriksonian measure developed by our research group was of Industry vs. Isolation, the stage preceding Identity. Andrea Kowaz (Kowaz and Marcia, 1991) devised a questionnaire measure for schoolchildren in grades 4–6 that covered cognitive, affective, and behavioral areas and assessed the extent to which children considered themselves able to realistically persevere at tasks. Children's scores were validated against both teachers' and parents' evaluations of children's Industry as well as several behavioral tasks. Children high in Industry were found generally to confirm Erikson's ideas that a child of this age should be able "To bring a productive situation to completion . . . which gradually supercedes the whims and wishes of play." (Erikson, 1963, 259)

Erikson's seventh psychosocial stage is Generativity/Stagnation. The life cycle issue involved here revolves around the concept of care—care for the life cycles of others and care for oneself. It involves also the generation of self-chosen projects as well as progeny. Cheryl Bradley (Bradley, 1997; Bradley and Marcia, 1998) developed a category measure of this stage using a semistructured interview and scoring manual. Criteria for placement in a Generativity status are involvement and inclusiveness. Involvement refers to one's behavioral and psychological investment in the lives and progress of the next generation; inclusiveness refers to who qualifies for one's care-giving activities. Those persons called Generative are invested actively in the life cycles of others as well as themselves. Their scope of care is broad and it takes into account both other's growth as well as the self's. While Agentically generative individuals care for others, they do so only to the extent that those others are involved in the Agentic person's own projects. If they become interested in other projects, including their own, the Agentic person's generativity ceases. Communally generative persons appear to be self-sacrificing in their care for others; however, their constant demands for gratitude and recognition from the recipient make the real object of their concern suspect. Those who are Conventionally generative extend themselves to care for others only so long as the objects of their care adhere to certain values and principles. While their care is not quite so self-centered as the Agentic individual's, the bandwidth of who qualifies for care is relatively narrow. Finally, Stagnant persons have little to offer in the way of either care for others, for themselves, or for their own projects.

The last stage in Erikson's theory involves the Integrity vs. Despair crisis of old age. As one approaches the end of one's life cycle, one may review one's life with either a general feeling of affirmation or of repudiation and regret. Whereas the scope of concern in the previous stage of Generativity was fairly restricted to one's own time and place, the scope in Integrity extends to all humankind, past and present. Simon Hearn (1993), and then Gary Saulnier (1998), developed and validated an interview measure of Integrity (Hearn, Saulnier, Strayer, Glenham, Koopman, and Marcia, under review). This measure located research participants aged seventy-two to ninety in one of four Integrity statuses using a scoring manual. Criteria for these groupings are: degree of conscious commitment (to values and a worldview); continuity from beliefs to actions (carrying through of the above beliefs and values into choices and actions in everyday life and relationships); connectedness (ongoing attachments with close others); and perspective (ability to look at self and others with candor and equanimity). Integrated persons have thought about who they are and how they became that way. They endorse both themselves and their world and maintain a sense of self through times of stress. They are aware and tolerant of more than one side of issues. Despair is not absent, but it is balanced by objective self-affirmation. Nonexploring individuals are often parochial and backward looking. The same boundaries that circumscribed their lives in late adolescence still apply. They have not engaged in a personal search for meaning, yet they can usually trust their instincts and feel generally positive about their lives. Despair is largely absent. Pseudo-integrated elders try to make their experiences fit into outmoded or simplistic and inadequate templates. The person they want to be and claim to be does not square with their presentation of themselves and their lives. There is a quality of brittleness and fragility, and even though Despair is not claimed, it seems to lurk just below the defensive surface. Despairing persons seem to have only minimal guidelines for living. They do not seem to understand persons or situations competently. They appear defeated and confused.

The foregoing is a very brief summary of the research work on Erikson's theory in which we have been engaged for more than thirty five years. To date there have been more than five hundred published studies and over one thousand dissertations on the identity research alone. There is now no question that Erikson's concepts can be defined operationally and validated empirically in numerous experimental situations. The nature of his language, which is more literary than scientific, did not make this task easy. But he did not set out to be a scientist—at least not in the *naturwissenshaft* mode. His was a more *geisteswissenshaft* approach. His misgivings about the trivialization of his concepts, in order to make them scientifically testable, are to some extent justified. One has to reduce pages of descriptive language to essential points in order to establish measurable criteria for resolution of a stage. However, because Erikson was a theorist and clinician, rather than a social scientist, he did not foresee that the temporary "shrinkage" of his concepts could eventually lead to their theoretical and empirical expansion and enrichment. By virtue of the nomological network (the established relationships between measures of his constructs and a host of correlated variables), we can add to his theoretical descriptions our empirically derived characteristics, thereby expanding his theory and linking it to other theories such as cognitive developmental, moral developmental, classical psychoanalytical, object relations, factor theory, etc. We could only have done this because his ideas had an inherent validity and were so clearly applicable to a wide range of human experience.

What is seldom talked about in doing research is whether or not it is "fun." By fun, I mean personally engaging, as well as interesting and meaningful. I do not think that so many students and colleagues would have embarked on what tended to be such time-consuming and complex scientific voyages had they not felt that these rich ideas were worth the trouble. Eriksonian research does not proceed easily and quickly. The concepts are complex and they involve the whole person at a particular point in the life cycle, rather than just isolated "traits." Hence, it has seemed to me that the labor-intensive interview rather than the more expedient questionnaire method is required to do justice to the concepts —and persons—under study. However, in order to meet the standards of scientific objectivity, this "subjective" interview method must be made objective, and that takes time and work. The payoff, besides a particular study's results, lies in the process itself. Each person interviewed emerges as an individual, coping in their own particular way with an important issue in their life cycle. Anyone giving Identity, Intimacy, Generativity, or

Integrity interviews emerges with not just an eventual "status" category, but a thumbnail sketch of an individual at a crisis point in their lives. It is the kind of research that enriches the researcher and the participant, as well as the body of psychological theory.

That a theory be capable of generating research is criterion enough for scientists. But as a psychotherapist and teacher, I wanted a theory that would carry over into these fields of practice as well. The next section will discuss some of the more practical implications of Erikson's psychosocial developmental approach.

Theory and Psychotherapy

I have grouped these two topics together because it is particularly in the structure of Erikson's (1963) theory that its most profound therapeutic implications lie. Before discussing that, I would like to address briefly the more obvious relationships between the content of Erikson's psychosocial developmental theory and psychotherapy. One of the most immediately apparent aspects is its dovetailing with classical psychoanalytic theory. This appears both in Erikson's emphasis on the somatic aspects of development and the resulting close correspondence between his first three stages of Trust, Autonomy, and Initiative and the associated classical psychosexual stages: oral, anal, and phallic/clitoral (oedipal). What Erikson added to the classical stages were both the ego developmental aspects and the importance of the social/cultural milieu within which these developmental issues were to be resolved. What would be the difference, then, if a psychotherapist operated more within Erikson's psychosocial developmental framework than within a more orthodox analytic one? While it is mostly a question of frame of mind, of a general outlook on the human condition, than it is of particular therapeutic techniques, there are some technical implications. If the social context is to be considered as truly meaningful and not just symbolic, if a broad, and multiple network of "causes" is to be considered, and if psychological determinism is to be explored within the context of individual construction, then a more active questioning technique than the interpretation of free associations is required. Psychotherapy within this framework, then, resembles more a mutual dialogue than it does a patient's production of associational material responded to with an analyst's interpretations.

Psychotherapists informed by Erikson tend to look more to issues of adaptation (see Hartmann, 1964) than to repetition of early conflicts. The past is important, but of equal importance is the current level and style of coping with predominant life cycle challenges as well as the pursuit of future goals. Conflict is still important, as it is within any psychodynamic approach, but the stage on which the conflicts are played out is much expanded. The conflicts are not just internal, but between alternative ways of being in the world, of being with oneself, of being with others. Also, the conflicts within the individual often mirror the conflicts of the culture. Although this perspective can certainly be derived from classical theory, it is at the heart of the Eriksonian approach which directs the practitioner's attention to the social/cultural contexts within which an individual's development takes place. This emphasis on past, present, and future, as well as context is illustrated by a first session I had recently with a forty-nine-year-old man. Because of his age, I was interested to know where he stood on Generativity. This particular individual had no children, so I knew that I must look elsewhere in his life for evidence. It turned out that he had been involved in training and mentoring activities within his occupational sphere of heavy machinery operation. I was interested in his Identity development, given that his father was a Scandinavian immigrant (and an alcoholic), and was also involved with machinery. My client's Identity picture was made more interestingly complex by his interest in art. The mechanical/artistic split emerged likewise in his art which consists of technical, draftsman-like work, on the one hand, and abstract figures of swirling colors, on the other. He had been through a surprising number of "jobs," none of which seemed to qualify as an occupation or vocation. And, like many of our Identity Diffusions, he felt acutely the lack of a validating father during his childhood and adolescence. I was interested in his style of Intimacy. He had been with his partner for twenty-nine years, so there was clearly some commitment there. But what of the depth of the relationship? His many jobs had taken him far from home for long periods of time. How had the couple negotiated this? Certainly, I shall explore his early conflicts and how they impact the present. But, I shall be interested also in his former and current strengths, in what he is doing well, and what impediments exist to his future. In a word, an Eriksonian approach *broadens* one's therapeutic perspective and techniques. In fact, using Erikson's scheme as a developmental outline with which to formulate a patient's dynamics, techniques borrowed from nonpsychodynamic orientations (e.g., cognitive-behavioral, gestalt, client-centered) may be used in furthering psychosocial developmental growth.

Earlier, I made a distinction between the content and the structure of Erikson's theory. By content, I mean the phase-specific developmental crises themselves. By structure, I mean the ways in which these periods are ordered. The form of Erikson's diagram provides the practitioner with some valuable therapeutic direction. What is often overlooked in the necessarily simplified presentation of Erikson's theory in undergraduate textbooks, is the fact that the developmental diagram consists of sixty-four, not just eight, squares. It is true that each of the eight chronological age periods have their own stage-specific issue that is predominant.

However, in addition to this primary issue, there are all of the seven other issues present, in some form, at every age. So, for example, during late adolescence, when the primary issue is Identity vs. Identity Confusion, there is a recurrence of Trust vs. Mistrust, Autonomy vs. Shame and Doubt, Initiative vs. Guilt, and Industry vs. Inferiority. In addition, at late adolescent Identity, there are preludes to eventual resolutions of young adult Intimacy vs. Isolation, middle-age Generativity vs. Stagnation, and old age Integrity vs. Despair. Hence, at any given age period, one is dealing with eight psychosocial issues, in some form, not just one. The implication this has for psychotherapy is that if one is at, say, young adulthood, and having difficulty with Intimacy, it is possible to look back into the life cycle to see just where the origins of this difficulty lie (perhaps Identity, perhaps Basic Trust) and then to address this preceding issue within the current context of the person's life. The theoretical assumption that every issue occurs at every age means that every issue can be resolved in some form at every age. Just because the optimal time for the resolution of, say, Autonomy (early childhood) is past does not mean that the late adolescent who is struggling with Identity issues because of previously unresolved Autonomy concerns, cannot resolve Autonomy during late adolescence, at the same time that Identity is being formulated. The forerunners to future stage-resolutions are also important. Consider the pregnant teenager who must deal not just with age-appropriate Identity issues, but also with the premature resolution of Intimacy and Generativity concerns. The theory allows for this possibility and directs the therapist to consider the precocious resolution of these later life cycle issues within the general context of the age-specific Identity issue.

The possibilities for the remediation of previously inadequately resolved developmental crises in ego growth, as well as the possibilities for the precocious resolution of later stages, adds a note of hopefulness to the outlook of the therapist practicing within an Eriksonian framework. True, the earlier the difficulty lies (e.g., Basic Trust) the more difficult the remediation, because subsequent stages are also likely to be flawed. Hence, one is dealing not just with the age-specific issue, but all of the previously unresolved issues as well. Also, it is a lot to expect of an eleven-year-old dying of cancer to attain some sense of Integrity. But the possibility of both of these exists within the theory. And the theory gives the practitioner some sense of direction.

Another difficulty the practitioner faces within psychosocially oriented psychotherapy is that the conditions, both individual and social, that were present when a stage was normally expected to be resolved no longer exist. Each chronological age has associated social institutions more or less keyed to individuals' needs at that age: mothering practices at infancy (Basic Trust); toilet-training customs at toddlerhood (Autonomy); elementary schools at middle childhood (Industry), etc. These are some of the "average expectable conditions" which Erikson and the ego psychologists said were necessary for optimal crisis resolution. There are no such institutions available for, say, a middle-aged adult who, in addition to dealing with Generativity, may be confronting earlier Autonomy issues. The world is not geared to providing the same kinds of supports and forgivenesses for a "responsible" adult than it is for cute toddlers. Hence, we invoke the "better-than-average expectable condition" of psychotherapy. The challenge facing the psychotherapist is how to deal with the toddler-age issue in the grown-up context of a middle-aged adult without either neglecting the child-based nature of the issue or infantilizing the adult patient. Again, because the Autonomy issue exists at *every* age, one can expect to be able to help the individual resolve Autonomy (and possibly subsequent childhood issues) within that person's adult context. Erikson's theory does not tell us *how* to do this (other theories of therapy are necessary here), but it does tell us that it can be done and also suggests other stage-specific issues that may have been impacted.

The recurrence of developmental issues throughout the life cycle is especially important in the case of Identity. This is because Identity, in contrast to other stage-specific issues has more of a structural quality. One can speak of "an" identity, but must refer to the other stages as "a sense of" say, Industry, Trust, etc. Once formed, an identity is subject to both continuity and change. One remains who one was, but also becomes different in response to bodily changes, the accumulation of life experience, and social expectations. There are likely to be identity reformulations at least at each succeeding life cycle period after adolescence (see Marcia, 2002). This puts so-called "midlife crises" in a somewhat different perspective. An identity crisis at midlife (as well as at young adulthood and old age) is to be expected from the form of the theory alone. Treating an adult undergoing an identity crisis in middle age as a normal expectable development removes some of the stigma associated with the popularly termed "midlife crisis" associated stereotypically with running the clock backward to slicker and younger partners, cars, and appearances. While crisis, conflict, and change in adult identity may not be celebrated by one's family and peers, it is a normally expectable occurrence and, if regarded positively and with some support, can be a growth-producing event.

Erikson's theory is not a theory of psychotherapy. It is a theory of ego development. It does not tell a practitioner what to do. Erikson was content to let standard psychoanalytic theory inform his clinical practice. What it does provide the practitioner is a kind of roadmap of development, of what can be reasonably expected, of where, developmentally, to intervene when difficulties arise, and at what level to intervene. Counseling techniques are most effective when the individual is dealing primarily with developmental issues at their expectable age-specific times, e.g.,

Identity at adolescence, Intimacy at young adulthood. Psychotherapeutic techniques, aimed at structural change (see Marcia 1999), are necessary when one must address previously unresolved stages; for example, Initiative at adolescence, Identity at young adulthood. In addition, the theory provides a set of reasonable therapeutic goals. One can expect a sense of Generativity to be developed at middle age, an Integrity resolution at old age. When this is accomplished, the therapy (or counseling) may be considered to be completed. Perhaps most importantly, Erikson's theory gives the psychotherapist a broad and reasonably optimistic framework through which to regard and to treat patients.

Not only has Erikson's theory been the source of a rich and generative application to psychological science and psychotherapy, it has also taught us much (and contributed much to our own teaching) about the human condition and development through life. As such, it has also, to my way of thinking, provided something of an outline for living.

An Outline for Living

Much of what I said previously about theory and psychotherapy applies as well in this section. Theories of personality abound. Having taught them to undergraduates and graduate clinical psychology students for a number of years, I am very aware of their differing perspectives on human nature, on what is possible for humankind to achieve. The classical Freudian position is that the best we can hope for is a kind of compromise between contradictory and ultimately unfulfillable desires, the external and internalized constraints of society, and our limited personal, executive resources (Rieff, 1979). The humanists, exemplified by Carl Rogers and Abraham Maslow, are much more optimistic about human potential, with joyous self-actualization being a realizable goal. Behaviorists and cognitive behaviorists eschew such long-range views and limit themselves to problem-solving, being willing to admit only that people, given the proper conditions, can change. "New Age" or "alternative therapies" advocates see an almost unlimited future for humankind; when one surveys the plethora of methods available and the claims made for them, one wonders how anyone could possibly still be unhappy. Yet enough of us are, enough of the time, that we become deeply suspicious of "remedies" and begin to think, with Freud, that unhappiness may be an essential part of the human condition.

Still, most of us know moments of happiness, moments of joy, moments of fulfillment (as well, of course, as moments of despair, sorrow, and helplessness.) It is those "in-between" times that make up the major part of our daily life, when we are more or less content or discontent, satisfied or dissatisfied, energetic and focused or apathetic and scattered, that a satisfactory theory of personality must address. The highs and lows, like the tides, will course through the channels of our lifetime, but we require an outlook that will keep us balanced between the ebbs and flows. What Erikson has given us is not just a theory for developmental psychologists, or sociologists, or psychotherapists, or psychohistorians, but a theory—an outline for living—within which we can understand ourselves and others. I do not think that students' resonance to Erikson's theory comes from my skills as a teacher. I think that it is a response to the inherent good sense of the theory itself. What Erikson has proposed is a schedule of development of strengths that are within the reach of almost everyone, even those living under what many of us would consider extreme conditions. Trust, Autonomy, Initiative, Industry, Identity, Intimacy, Generativity, and Integrity are qualities that would be recognized by all peoples at all times as desirable and possible. Their development depends primarily upon a certain quality of interrelationships between parents and children, teachers and students, romantic partners, and social institutions and individuals. Erikson referred to those interrelationships as the "cog-wheeling" of individuals' needs and abilities and the milieu's provision of rewards and demands. The theory does not propose transcendence or transformation, although it does not exclude these. It is a theory grounded in the heroics of everyday life.

As to whether or not the theory is "cross-cultural," I would say first that this is an empirical question, one which is being partially answered by identity research being carried on every continent. Secondly, Erikson took care to look at non-technological societies (Erikson, 1963) in his formulation of his developmental schedule. Finally, I would make an appeal to common sense. All humans begin life as infants who are wholly dependent upon caregivers (Trust). Socialization of impulses is an essential aspect of child-rearing in all societies (Autonomy). Sex roles, incest taboos, and the resultant internalization of social standards are universal (Initiative). All cultures train their young in the particular technology of the culture, whether that involves reading and writing, computer literacy, or fashioning hunting implements and learning agricultural skills (Industry). The marking of the coming of age at adolescence, the acknowledgement of childhood's end and adulthood's beginning, occurs more or less formally all over the world (Identity). Courtship and mating and the institutions surrounding them are part of all human experience (Intimacy). Children and younger members of society require care from adults (Generativity). Yet, everyone, if they live long enough, experiences physical decline and must face death (Integrity). Although, from culture to culture, and era to era, some specific content may change, and the timing of the psychosocial stages may differ, as well, the social institutions provided for their resolution may vary, one would have to deny very fundamental aspects of being human in order to deny the universality of relevance of Erikson's theory.

Returning again to the theme of the form, as contrasted with the content, of the theory, some of the genius of the theory, and its resonance with lived life, is to be found in its smaller details. I would like to discuss two of these in the following paragraphs: the use of "versus (vs.)" (e.g., Basic Trust *vs.* Mistrust, Integrity *vs.* Despair, etc.) when defining each stage; and the importance of the "negative" aspects of the stage resolutions (e.g., Inferiority, Isolation, Stagnation, etc.)

The more research we did on the Eriksonian stages, the more I struggled with Erikson's concept of "versus" in describing the stage-specific crises in ego growth. The term suggested to me a kind of dichotomous either-or position. That is, one had either a sense of Autonomy or a sense of Guilt and Shame; one was either Generative or Stagnant. We knew from studying stage resolutions from late adolescence onward that there were not just two alternatives but, rather, different *styles* of being, say, Intimate or Integrated. It seemed, especially, with the development of formal operations and sophisticated self-reflectiveness in late adolescence, that our research participants were "doing" the stage resolutions in discriminably different forms. They were not just high or low, resting on one pole or the other. Furthermore, placement along a continuum seemed to better reflect the pre-adolescent stages. Our schoolchildren could be fairly accurately described as tending more toward Industry or toward Inferiority.[3] And younger children seemed to be more or less trusting, autonomous, or initiating. So, given that pre-adolescents seemed most accurately described as being along a continuum, and post-adolescents seemed most accurately described as manifesting different styles of stage resolution, how accurate was a "vs." designation?

My first solution to this was to use "and" rather than "versus," particularly as applied to the adolescent and adult stages, for example, Identity and Identity Diffusion, Intimacy and Isolation, etc. Each of the styles (statuses) that we employed in measuring these stages had elements of both poles of the stage-specific crisis, save, of course, for the least successful resolutions (e.g., Diffusion, Isolation, etc.). In order to incorporate these least successful resolutions, I then again changed the stage designations to the form of Basic Trust/Mistrust, Integrity/Despair, etc. I thought that that would adequately indicate the issue with which the individual was dealing without suggesting an either-or solution or imposing a mixed resolution when no such mixture was apparent. Most recently, especially in listening to, and thinking about, our oldest respondents, I have become convinced of the wisdom of Erikson's original formulation. The word "versus" connotes so well the sense of crisis and change that is an essential element in growth. Every stage resolution contains an element of personal risk and loss, an opportunity for advance or decline, for inertia or momentum. Looking just at our older people, they are forced to deal in some way with declining physical capabilities and changed social expectations. They experience themselves, and are experienced by others, as different from their middle-aged selves. Although this is more acute in our youth-oriented culture, older people in every culture must deal with a diminution in physical, and sometimes mental, strength. One may deny these changes, succumb to them, or somehow integrate them into the selves that they will carry into their foreshortened future. At no time in the life cycle is there change and growth without loss. And loss is painful. The infant, totally dependent on its caretakers, need not (cannot), care for itself, and, in the best of circumstances, can rely wholly on a benevolent and nurturant environment. But its built-in growth propels it into a crisis of autonomy—of having to make choices, even if those choices are such elementary ones as when and where to eliminate the waste products of its body. Young adults, having made the commitments necessary to establish an identity, find themselves having to modify that sometimes hard-won identity in order to make an intimate relationship with another individual who is having to modify *their* perhaps equally hard-won identity. Older people, having labored long in the fields of generativity, caring for others and their own life projects, now find themselves having to withdraw to some extent from these activities in order to preserve their energies for what "really counts." And they can no longer pretend that all of their life decisions were wise ones. How can one both acknowledge and bear one's mistakes and still affirm "one's one-and-only life cycle"? Slipping into Shame and Doubt lurk as a real danger for the infant transitioning to early childhood. Isolation is a real possibility for the young adult unable or unwilling to modify an identity. Despair looms for the elder who confronts recollections of life errors on one side and impending death on the other. I now think that Erikson's term, "versus," is the best description for psychosocial developmental crises, with their possibilities for regression, stagnation, or progression.

The "negative" poles of the psychosocial stage resolutions are typically presented as largely undesirable outcomes. They are so, if they remain unmixed with the "positive" pole. But they serve as a useful reminder that Erikson's developmental schedule does not entail just climbing up a psychosocial achievement ladder. It is the *integration* of the negative aspects involved in psychological growth that adds a realistic and existential quality to Erikson's theory. Experience-based Mistrust, appropriate Shame and Doubt, self-correcting Guilt, reality-oriented Inferiority, flexible Identity Diffusion, potentially self-affirming Isolation, possibly regeneratively fallow Stagnation, and hard-nosed Despair—all are necessary complements to the "brighter" side of the positive stage resolutions. Without the acknowledgment and incorporation of these shadows, essential aspects of humanness would be absent. All of our adolescent and adult status descriptions involve an admixture of the negative pole into even the most positive resolutional styles.

Why Erikson?

In this essay, I have tried to answer this question both for the reader and for myself. Erikson's theory has provided me, as well as some of my students and my colleagues, an investigative platform for our lifetimes. Although his ideas were initially cast in a far-from-operational form, they have proved measurable and valid. This research work continues today. As of this writing, we are awaiting an editorial review of our new measure of Integrity vs. Despair. The Identity concept, in particular, has been extraordinarily useful in understanding adolescent development and in inspiring hundreds of studies. Although Erikson's is not a theory of psychotherapy, it is a comprehensive framework within which psychotherapists of many theoretical persuasions can carry out their work. It does not tell them what to do—other theories and techniques are available for that—but it does tell them where their clients might be coming from, where they are currently, and where they might be expected to go. It is not a vehicle, but it is a superb map. There are no theories of personality that provide such a comprehensive overview of the human life cycle, emphasizing both realistic possibilities and potential pitfalls. It is, above all, a thoroughgoingly human portrait in which all peoples, everywhere, can find themselves portrayed. As a psychotherapist, and as a person, who views on one side the cognitive behavioral technicians and sees on the other starry-eyed "spiritual healers," I find Erikson solid ground on which I can stand in order to understand the scope and course of human development, my patients, and myself.

Notes

1. Joan Erikson, I have heard, was more kindly disposed.
2. By doing so, I do not mean to ignore the good work of other investigators. For example, I do not think that the identity statuses, as an approach to conceptualizing identity, are "the alpha and omega" of identity research as one investigator has suggested (McAdams 1996, in response to Marcia and Strayer 1996). His own research, as well as that of several others, have made substantial contributions to understanding different facets of Erikson's complex identity concept. That the identity status research is the most frequently cited does not necessarily

58	*Marcia*

make it the "alpha" approach, but rather one that has opened doors to further perceptions and considerations of the richness of Erikson's theory.

3. Although even here, there were some children who seemed "industrious" but were so in a very driven way that we felt betokened a compensatory reaction to a fear of inferiority. This possibility has remained largely unexplored empirically.

References

Bartholomew, K., A. J. Z. Henderson, and J. E. Marcia. "Coding Semi-Structured Interviews in Social Psychological Research," in *Handbook of Research Methods in Social and Personality Psychology*, eds. Harry T. Reis and Charles M. Judd, New York: Cambridge University Press, 2000.

Bradley, C. L. "Generativity-Stagnation: Development of a Status Model," *Developmental Review* 17, no. 3 (1997): 262–90.

Bradley, C. L. and J. E. Marcia. "Generativity-Stagnation: A Five Category Model," *Journal of Personality* 66, no. 1 (1998): 39–64.

Erikson, E. H. "Identity and the Life Cycle," *Psychological Issues*, Monograph No. 1. New York: International Universities Press, 1959.

———. *Childhood and Society*, 2nd rev. ed., New York: Norton, 1963.

Gilligan, C. *In a Different Voice: Psychological Theory and Women's Development*. Cambridge, MA: Harvard University Press, 1982.

Hartmann, H. *Essays on Ego Psychology*. New York: International Universities Press, 1964.

Hearn, S. *Integrity, Despair, and in Between: Toward Construct Validation of Erikson's Eighth Stage*. Unpublished doctoral dissertation, Simon Fraser University, Burnaby, British Columbia, Canada, 1993.

Hearn, S., G. Saulnier, J. Strayer, M. Glenham, R. Koopman, and J. E. Marcia. "Between Integrity and Despair: Toward Construct Validation of Erikson's Eighth Stage." Department of Psychology, Simon Fraser University, Burnaby, British Columbia, Canada (under review).

Kelly, G. *The Psychology of Personal Constructs*. 2 vols. New York: Norton, 1955.

Kohlberg, L. "Moral Stages and Moralization: The Cognitive Developmental Approach," in *Moral Development and Moral Behavior*, ed. T. Lickona. New York: Holt, Rinehart and Winston, 1976.

Kowaz, A. M. and J. E. Marcia. "Development and Validation of a Measure of Eriksonian Industry," *Journal of Personality and Social Psychology* 60, no. 3 (1991): 390–97.

Marcia, J. E. "Representational Thought in Ego Identity, Psychotherapy, and Psychosocial Developmental Theory," in *Development of Mental Representation: Theories and Applications,* ed. Irving E. Sigel. Mahwah, NJ: L. E. Erlbaum, 1999.

———. "Identity and psychosocial development in adulthood. *Identity: An International Journal of Theory and Research* 2, no. 1 (2002), 7–29.

Marcia, J. E. and J. Strayer. "Theories and Stories," *Psychological Inquiry: An International Journal of Peer Commentary and Review* 7, no. 4 (1996): 346–50.

Marcia, J. E., A. S. Waterman, D. R. Matteson, S. L. Archer, and J. L. Orlofsky. *Ego Identity: A Handbook for Psychosocial Research.* New York: Springer-Verlag, 1993.

McAdams, D. P. "Personality, Modernity, and the Storied Self: A Contemporary Framework for Studying Persons," *Psychological Inquiry: An International Journal of Peer Commentary and Review* 7, no. 4 (1996): 295–322.

Orlofsky, J. L., J. E. Marcia, and I. M. Lesser. "Ego Identity Status and the Intimacy Versus Isolation Crisis of Young Adulthood," *Journal of Personality and Social Psychology* 27 (1973): 211–19.

Rieff, Phillip. *Freud: The Mind of the Moralist,* 3rd ed. Chicago: University of Chicago Press, 1979.

Saulnier, G. *Maturation of Thought: Advanced Construct Validation of Erikson's Eighth Stage.* Unpublished doctoral dissertation, Simon Fraser University, Burnaby, British Columbia, Canada, 1998.

Skoe, E. E. and J. E. Marcia. "The Development and Partial Validation of a Care-Based Measure of Moral Development," *Merrill-Palmer Quarterly,* 37 (1991): 289–304.

Chapter Five

Identity in Formation

Jane Kroger

An individual life cycle cannot be adequately understood apart from the social context in which it comes to fruition. Individual and society are intricately woven, dynamically related in continual change.

— Erik Erikson, *Identity and the Life Cycle*, p. 114

Erikson's own personal life history and its intersection with the cultural and historical contexts in which he lived and worked enabled the psychoanalyst to bring the construct of ego identity into vivid focus. It was primarily through identity's absence that Erikson, both personally and professionally, was able to identify and illuminate that entity which gives form and shape to human existence. When functioning well, identity can be taken for granted; when absent, it appears as a complex achievement (Erikson, 1975). Identity is also formed in interaction with a historical context. And it was perhaps to that North American nation of immigrants, struggling to attain a sense of place in society as well as a sense of coherence in their own lives, that Erikson's writings on identity spoke particularly well. In turn, a nation of immigrants provided for this particular immigrant a crucial context of acceptance and appreciation.

I first met Erikson as a very old man. Yet the identity themes that had so preoccupied his earlier writings still were apparent in his understandings of life's concluding times. I was part of a small seminar group meeting fortnightly in the Eriksons' Cambridge home, and that seminar became a type of professional "life review" through many of Erikson's early and later published and unpublished works. The seminar had attracted clinicians, theologians, academic psychologists, and students from several nations. And though we worked in many languages and had varied reasons for our presence, the depth of Erikson's concepts spoke to us all.

In this chapter, I review some of the many important concepts that Erikson contributed to an understanding of identity and its initial formative process, noting a few of the varied criticisms that Erikson received in relation to these groundbreaking insights. I then turn briefly to overview of some of the contributions more recent researchers have made to an understanding of identity in its initial formation during adolescence. On the basis of some of my own qualitative investigations into identity revision and maintenance processes of late adulthood, I then propose possible ongoing processes of identity development over adult life, to extend the initial groundwork that Erikson began. In conclusion, I hope to stimulate future identity researchers into a deeper exploration of identity's formation and reformation processes over time.

What Is Identity?

Erikson first used the concept of ego identity to describe a central disturbance in the functioning of some World War II veterans returning from battle: "What impressed me most was the loss in these men of a sense of identity. They knew who they were; they had a personal identity. But it was as if subjectively, their lives no long hung together—and never would again. There was a central disturbance in what I then started to call ego identity" (Erikson, 1963, 42). He continued later by noting that we become most aware of identity when just about to gain it or when it is called into question (Erikson, 1968). Thus, through its absence, Erikson was able to delineate identity's central elements, bringing them into clear relief.

Among the most critical of identity's properties, Erikson noted, is its provision for a sense of continuity and self-sameness essential to a satisfying human existence. Despite changes in interpersonal relationships, social roles, and contexts, an attained sense of identity enables one to experience a continued sense of self and role commitments across time and place. "Even with all the changes in my marriages, family, other relationships and work circumstances, I'm still me. I just keep on growing and finding better options for self-expression and better places for support," commented one thirty-year-old student, participating in a study of identity during adulthood (Kroger, 2000, unpublished raw data). Identity is both a state of being and becoming, a quality of unselfconscious living for those in its possession. However, this sense of individual continuity must also be paired with one's appreciation of the sameness and continuity of some shared world image in order for optimal identity functioning to occur (Erikson, 1975). Identity is partly conscious but also partly unconscious in form, as it provides that vital continuity for human existence.

Erikson also gave us new insights into the biological, psychological, and social properties of identity. Later, he also added historical context as a further determinant of identity. Identity's attainment enables the individual, with all of his or her own biological givens, psychological interests, aptitudes, needs, and defenses, to find satisfying vocational, ideological, and relational roles within a particular social setting during a particular historical epoch. Simply stated, identity provides one with a sense of well-being—a sense of being at home in one's body, a sense of direction to one's life, and a sense of mattering to those who count. Identity is what makes one move with direction; identity is what gives one reason to be.

Identity normatively becomes a focus of concern during adolescence. With newfound cognitive and physical abilities in contexts which now began to hold expectations for the assumption of adult responsibilities, the growing individual encounters a widening range of identity options— at least in contexts where choice is allowed. Identity in adolescence, to Erikson (1963), involves a new integration of previous childhood identifications with current individual endowments and opportunities provided by available social roles in the surrounding milieu. Identity achievement gives rise to a new configuration, greater than the sum of its individual parts. Where such integration is unsuccessful, identity confusion arises. Erikson suggested that it is the inability to settle on an occupation that most preoccupies youth. A more or less favorable resolution to Erikson's task of Identity vs. Role Confusion is possible only through more or less favorable resolutions to preceding psychosocial tasks of infancy and childhood: Trust vs. Mistrust, Autonomy vs. Doubt and Shame, Initiative vs. Guilt, and Industry vs. Inferiority.

Erikson (1968) elaborated the important relationship between identity and identification, concepts with common linguistic as well as psychological roots, but with great differences in meaning and implications. A functioning adolescent and adult identity, for Erikson, could never result from the mere summation of childhood identifications. Yet, identifications serve as important foundations for later identity. Identification is the process by which children and other individuals aspire to be like or to take on roles and appearances of significant others. Children thus begin to build a set of expectations of what they wish to be and do in times ahead.

The process of identity formation begins when merely adopting the roles and personality attributes of significant others no longer satisfies one. Identity, rather, ". . . arises from the selective repudiation and mutual assimilation of childhood identifications and their absorption in a new configuration . . ." (Erikson, 1968, 159). This new identity configuration irreversibly alters previous identifications of childhood. Individual identity is furthermore dependent for its formation and fulfillment upon psychosocial forces. An individual's recognition of the social context to which he or she chooses to engage intertwined with that community's response to the newly evolving individual provide the cornerstones for identity.

For some individuals, identity struggles hold center stage well beyond adolescence. Certain psychological and/or social factors may conspire to prolong an individual's identity resolution. Erikson noted that for some highly gifted and creative individuals, there may be a prolonged search for appropriate vocational and ideological niches. His psychobiographical accounts of Martin Luther and Mahatma Gandhi illustrate how individual psychological needs (in both of these cases, a childhood "account" to settle) may become writ large over the pages of history. Erikson (1964, 204) also pointed out how certain social conditions, such as times of rapid social change, may produce widespread identity vacua, wherein a sudden sense of alienation becomes widespread. "Some periods in history become identity vacua caused by the three basic forms of human apprehension: fears . . . ; anxieties . . . ; and . . . dread . . . ." By the same token, however, such historical eras present the opportunity for social renewal through the emergence of new leadership possibilities and new collective strategies for adaptation.

A further important property of identity to Erikson is its evolving nature. For Erikson, the identity established at the end of adolescence provides some foundation for entry into adult life. However, identity continues to evolve throughout adulthood. "In fact, each subsequent stage of adulthood must contribute to [identity's] preservation and renewal" (Erikson, 1975, 19). Erikson has elaborated the establishment of a sense of identity in adolescence in some detail; however, he has been less vocal on how exactly identity continues to evolve beyond this normative time of initial resolution.

Erikson's contributions to an understanding of identity have not been without criticism (see Hoare, 2002, for an excellent review of Erikson's critics). One important point of contention raised by critics and acknowledged by Erikson himself, was that by drawing upon concepts from several disciples, Erikson became master of none. "I do not have the knowledge necessary to approach in any systematic fashion the relationship between ego qualities, social institutions, and historical eras" (Erikson, 1963, 279). Writing at the intersection of disciplines, however, provided numerous fresh perspectives on identity that could not emerge from within any single discipline alone.

Erikson has also been greatly criticized for the vagueness in many of his concepts as well as in his writing style. Erikson sometimes referred to his important identity concept as a structure or configuration, at other times as a process. Sometimes identity was viewed as a conscious, subjective experience, at other times as an unconscious entity. Erikson's opaque and sometimes contradictory accounts of this single concept have evoked much critical comment as well. Again, Erikson responded with a candid statement during one radio interview broadcast: "I think one could be more precise than I am, or than I am able to be. I very much feel that scientific training and logic would have helped a lot" (Erikson, cited in Stevens, 1983, 112). At the same time, Erikson (1975) defended the many faces of identity he created by arguing that all were necessary in order to understand how individuals maintained and retained a sense of continuity and wholeness in a world of contending forces.

Erikson's writing style is nonlinear. As an artist, he tended to paint impressions through his prose, rather than develop clear logic in his literary style. Finding theoretical validity through his many poetic associations has often proved an anathema for those in search of a logical progression of arguments. Despite these and other difficulties, however, Erikson has expanded our understanding of personality development well beyond adolescence and has provided many identity-related concepts in need of further empirical study.

Identity in Formation

Given the varied properties of identity, how does it form? Erikson offered many thoughts on identity's initial formation. The identity formation process of adolescence involves the creation of a new psychological structure capable of constructing, rather than assuming the admired identity elements of another. This new configuration enables explorations of many new vocational, ideological, and relational possibilities, *on the individual's own terms*. Identity formation allows the individual to assess personal attributes and interests and to match these with outlets for expression available in his or her social milieu.

The integration now taking place in the form of ego identity is, as pointed out, more than the sum of the childhood identifications. It is the accrued experience of the ego's ability to integrate all identifications with the vicissitudes of the libido, with the aptitudes developed out of endowment, and with the opportunities offered in social roles" (Erikson, 1963, 216).

Subjectively, identity formation is the experience of adopting meaningful roles and values that make one feel and act "most like oneself." Conversely, identity confusion is the subjective experience of betraying one's "real" self. Observable dimensions of an identity in formation are an individual's ability to develop and maintain realistic commitments to particular social roles and values that "fit." For this reason, Erikson finds the ego virtue of fidelity—that ability to remain true to one's commitments despite difficulties—to be a hallmark of the identity achieved. Identity formation is an evolving, deepening sense of psychosocial commitment and of knowing what is worthy of one's fidelity in this world of many possibilities.

Social context plays a critical role in the identity formation process. Erikson invariably discusses the relationship between individual and social milieu in identity's evolution: "We deal with a process [identity formation] 'located' in the core of the individual and yet also in the core of [his/her] communal culture . . ." (Erikson, 1968, 22). The sense of fulfillment that emerges through successful resolutions to the identity formation process of adolescence is intimately linked with the recognition and type of response provided by the social milieu. The social context, in turn, is often enriched, often changed by the recognition and responsiveness of adolescing individuals in its care. The importance of context to later identity formation begins in infancy. That sense of "I," the foundation for identity's later evolution, can emerge only in the presence of an interested "other." And throughout ensuing years, it is the mutuality of recognition and responsiveness from others that enables both individual identity evolution as well as social change. Social contexts both shape and are shaped by identities in formation.

Since the time of Erikson's theoretical writings on identity, social scientists have been preoccupied with operationalizing and assessing identity's characteristics and developments. While many approaches to operationalizing identity have evolved, one popular model, drawn directly from elements of Erikson's theory, is the identity status framework proposed by James Marcia (Marcia, 1966, 1967; Marcia et al., 1993). Erikson had conceptualized identity as the attainment of a place along a continuum ranging between the two poles of identity achievement and role confusion. However, Marcia conceptualized identity in terms of several qualitatively distinct possibilities for resolution. He used the variables of exploration and commitment to define different styles by which late adolescents undertake various identity-defining decisions.

Four identity styles (or identity statuses) arose from the different combinations of these two variables: *identity achievement, moratorium, foreclosure, and diffusion.* Those in the identity achieved and foreclosed statuses were both firmly committed to identity-defining roles and values. However, the identity achieved had undertaken serious vocational, ideological, and relational commitments following a time of active exploration among alternative possibilities to find niches in society that really seemed to "fit" their own interests and abilities. The foreclosures, by contrast, had formed their commitments on the basis of identification, by adopting the roles and values that significant others had held, without active exploration of other possibilities on their own terms. Moratorium and identity diffuse individuals were similarly uncommitted to social role or value possibilities; yet they differed in a fundamental way from the identity diffuse. Moratoriums were very much in the process of active identity exploration, of looking at various options available within their contexts for vocational, ideological, and relational commitments, while the diffusions were not. Adolescents who were identity diffuse were unable, unwilling, and/or uninterested in making identity-defining commitments. These four types of adolescent identity resolution first identified by Marcia have been associated with various personality variables, familial antecedents, and developmental patterns of change (Marcia et al., 1993; Kroger, 2003). Of particular relevance here are findings from studies of the identity formation process itself.

At least two dozen researches adopting Marcia's identity status model have examined developmental features of identity during and beyond the years of adolescence (see Kroger, 2003, for a summary of these researches and a fuller discussion of key findings). These investigations have used longitudinal, cross-sectional, and retrospective methods e.g., Archer, 1982; Cramer, 1998; Fitch and Adams, 1983; Josselson, 1996; Kroger, 1995; Kroger and Haslett, 1987; Marcia, 1976; Waterman, Geary, and Waterman, 1974; Waterman and Goldman, 1976. The investigations have been conducted primarily in North America, though several have also been undertaken in Europe and the Pacific Basin.

Several interesting findings have emerged across studies. Firstly, for *all* longitudinal, cross-sectional, and retrospective studies only about half of the individuals who participated were rated identity achieved by time of entry into young adult life (about age twenty-one to twenty-two years). This result occurred, whether identity was rated in overall terms or by individual identity domains (vocation, ideology, relationships). There appears to be considerable scope for identity development beyond adolescence. From these same investigations, the primary pattern of movement for those who did change identity status was from a less mature (foreclosure or diffusion) to a more mature (moratorium or achieved) identity position. This finding is in accordance with Erikson's description of the stages of ego growth in the identity formation process of adolescence. Empirical results suggest that identity moves from a configuration based on identifications (the foreclosure position) to a new, more differentiated structure based on individual choice (the identity achieved position). Retrospective, and some longitudinal, studies indicate this movement occurs via a moratorium process. Longitudinal studies of identity status in late adolescence, however, have generally made assessments at one to three year intervals. Future longitudinal identity status research needs assessments that are undertaken at more frequent time intervals in order to provide a detailed understanding of movement patterns.

Surprisingly little research has been conducted on social conditions associated with various identity status resolutions during adolescence. Among those investigations of such relationships, it has been difficult to determine the direction of the effects. Is an individual with a particular identity status resolution drawn to contexts with certain types of features, or do certain types of contexts encourage the development of particular identity status resolutions? Do adolescents with certain types of identity structures elicit certain types of parental behaviors, or do certain types of parental behaviors promote particular types of identity structures among adolescents? Researches below indicate a strong relationship between identity and environment. At present however, one must be cautious about stating the primary direction of effects. What appears likely from researches to date is that social circumstances set broad limits to human behaviors, but individual personality characteristics play a key role in influencing the course of identity development over time (Kroger and Haslett, 1987; 1991).

Within the familial context, patterns of family communication have varied for adolescents within the different identity statuses. Parents of both identity-achieved and moratorium adolescents have tended to stress both individuality and connectedness in family relationships e.g., Campbell, Adams, and Dobson, 1984. Parents of moratoriums have also stressed independence in their child-rearing patterns e.g., Campbell et al., 1984. Those adolescent foreclosed have reported that their families are very close and child-centered; when the mother is too close, involved, and protective of her daughter, the daughter mirrors parental values rather than exploring other possibilities e.g., Perosa, Perosa, and Tam, 1996. Less reported conflict in families has also been associated with the foreclosed identity status e.g., Willemsen and Waterman, 1991. Parents who discourage the expression of individual opinions among family members have adolescents who exhibit very low levels of identity exploration e.g., Grotevant and Cooper, 1985. Adolescent diffusions have often reported distant or rejecting caretakers and generally low levels of attachment to their parents e.g., Campbell et al., 1984; Josselson, 1996.

Beyond the family, investigators have explored the impact of educational and wider community contexts on the identity formation process of adolescence. Fitch and Adams (1983), for example, found that certain university departmental environments seemed to attract students with particular characteristics, but once students were in departments, there were different factors that emerged to facilitate the identity formation process. Societal awareness, encouraged by faculty or peers, was one condition that helped students to broaden their perspectives on identity-related issues. Kroger and Haslett (1987, 1991) found that when situational variables such as age, level of education, socioeconomic status, and marital and parental status were controlled in a retrospective study of identity development by midlife adults, participants still demonstrated very different patterns of identity development during and beyond adolescence. Exposure to new contexts and internal change processes were the two primary factors associated with the identity formation process of late adolescence. In addition, major identity changes after adolescence were less likely to occur in association with contextual circumstances and more likely to occur in conjunction with internal change processes (Kroger and Green, 1996). These and a limited number of other identity status researches point to how individuals, in the identity formation process, draw upon their individually unique capacities in differential response to their social milieus (e.g., Berzonsky, 1994; Tesch and Cameron, 1987). Erikson, himself, noted "... *different capacities use different opportunities* to become full-grown components of the ever-new configuration that is the growing personality" (Erikson, 1959, 57; emphasis original).

Identity beyond Adolescence

In contrast to his extensive writings on the adolescent identity formation process, Erikson has not offered detailed comments on identity's ongoing evolution throughout adult life. Beyond adolescence, identity "... is always changing and developing: at its best it is a process of increasing differentiation, and it becomes ever more inclusive as the individual grows aware of a widening circle of others significant to [him/her], from the maternal person to "[humankind]" (Erikson, 1968, 23). While Erikson, Erikson, and Kivnick (1986) did undertake a qualitative examination of identity development in old age, they did not attempt to detail specific processes involved in identity's ongoing development.

Erikson has indicated that identity remains an active ingredient of adulthood psychosocial tasks of Intimacy vs. Isolation, Generativity vs. Stagnation, and Integrity vs. Despair. The challenge of Intimacy vs. Isolation in young adulthood can be met successfully only when there are two identities fairly firmly in place. Generativity in midlife depends upon the evolution of identity and fidelity to appropriate outlets for the care and enhancement of future generations. Integrity in old age is dependent upon the acceptance of identity choices and decisions made within one's one-and-only life cycle. Beyond these statements, however, Erikson has provided few details of identity's formation or reformation in adult life or of those social conditions most supportive of ongoing identity development. He has been heavily criticized even for extending his comments on identity development beyond the years of adolescence (Hoare, 2002).

How then might some of the processes so vital to adolescent identity formation continue to evolve during adulthood? Following a recent review of the scant literature on identity issues of late adulthood, I became fascinated with how exploration and commitment processes, described as central to adolescent identity formation by both .Erikson and Marcia, might continue to evolve during adult life. I undertook a small, exploratory study of identity development during late adulthood to learn more about how identity may be formed, reformed, and/or maintained across the many years of adulthood and to provide a stimulus for future research. Insights presented in the paragraphs that follow come through a series of life-history interviews I conducted with fourteen New Zealand men and women in their late adulthood years (Kroger, 2001). Eight of the individuals (four men and four women) were in their "younger" years of late adulthood (from sixty-five to seventy-five years), and six were in their "older" years (over seventy-six) of late adulthood (two men and four women). All lived in circumstances in which either they or their partner had held a professional or managerial work role prior to retirement (and thus were less likely to have experienced serious financial impediments to identity decisions). Individuals were contacted via a "networking" technique, and those with severe cognitive impairments were precluded from further study. It must be noted that all individuals who participated in this investigation would most likely have been assessed as identity achieved at some point during late adolescence or their earlier years of adult life.

    I found parallels to adolescent identity exploration and commitment processes in adult identity revision and maintenance undertakings. Among later-life adults who participated in my investigation, ongoing identity "exploration" was characterized by processes of reintegration, reevaluation, and refinement of important identity elements from the past as well as readjustments to the inevitable changes that life brings. *Reintegration* was a process of reweaving back into the fabric of life important identity elements that had been set aside for various reasons before it became "too late." Sometimes important identity elements had been set aside in the urgency of other responsibilities, at other times ignored because of their painful associations. Really meaningful identity elements, however, did not go away but rather only increasingly pressed for attention in life's latest stage, at least for the individuals of this investigation. *Reevaluation* was a process of rebalancing vocational and relational roles, particularly in the early stages of late adulthood. Vocationally and relationally, individuals were trying out new and discarding old roles, and shifting time investments and balances among various options. For the older old, there were often reconsiderations of life's meanings and a refocusing of one's energies. *Refinement* also occurred in relation to vocational and social roles, as individuals fine-tuned identity-defining commitments to best suit their changing abilities and life circumstances. *Readjustment* was a further identity revision process that accompanied major life changes, brought by various forms of change, particularly loss.

    "Commitment" or identity maintenance processes for these individuals included "tying up the package," establishing visible forms of continuity with previous interests, roles, and relationships, narrowing the boundaries of both physical and social worlds, and committing oneself more fully to living in the present. The younger old were often engaged in an identity maintenance process I called *"tying up the package."* This process involved integrating the important experiences of a lifetime into one single, creative work—often a book of memoirs, poems, newspaper accounts, and/or a collection of meaningful photographs or other artifacts. "Tying up the package" is different from leaving a legacy, an important dimension of generativity described by Erikson (1963), for "the package's" intended audience was primarily other family members. *Establishing visible forms of continuity* engaged the attentions of most late adulthood participants. Often important objects were retained through changed life circumstances as reminders of people and places that once were. For the older old, *a narrowing of physical and/or social boundaries* often occurred in efforts to best maintain and express important identity-defining interests, roles and values. Particularly among the older old, simply *living in the present* was an adaptive identity-maintenance stance that enhanced life's quality and pleasure. In this exploratory study, a different mix of these processes often punctuated early and later years of late adulthood. Among those in early late adulthood, identity reintegration and re-evaluation were the most common "exploration" processes, while identity refinements and readjustments predominated in the older age group.

Erikson (1968) suggested that vocation, ideology, and relationships are the most important psychosocial issues around which identity decisions crystallize during adolescence. Interestingly, most of these same identity-defining arenas were still salient for the late-adulthood participants interviewed here, though some additional themes also appeared. Concerns of vocational and relational rebalancing, and adjusting to family, friendship, and community roles all preoccupied the attentions of the younger old. During very late adulthood, identity-defining themes of considering one's own life meaning(s) and the refocusing of family and sometimes community role commitments were preoccupying concerns.

Directions for the Future

Erikson has provided many valuable insights into the construct of ego identity (1963, 1968). He emphasized the mutual interplay between individual and society in the formation of identity and has delineated some of identity's central properties. As a provider of continuity and a feeling of self-sameness, identity is central to a satisfying human existence. As a subjective experience, identity is what gives one a reason to be. As a configuration, identity undergoes a change of structure such that it comes to mediate rather than be mediated by the environment. It normatively becomes a concern of central importance during adolescence, when the so-cial milieu begins to press for one's engagement in psychosocial roles, and individual biological and psychological factors make responses to such processes both desirable and desired. Erikson also provided some general thoughts on identity's ongoing development over the years of adult life.

From themes noted in the preceding section, identity revision and maintenance processes do seem to occur throughout adult life. While identity may be "a process of increasing differentiation" and become more expansive as Erikson indicates, this process is also likely to involve somewhat more complex mechanisms than Erikson suggests. Identity revision in adulthood may involve reintegration, re-evaluation, and re-finement of important identity elements from the past, as well as read-justments to change, particularly loss. Identity maintenance in adulthood may involve "tying up the package," establishing visible forms of continu-ity with previous interests, roles, and relationships, narrowing the boundaries of both physical and social worlds, and committing oneself more fully to living in the present. Important identity-defining psychoso-cial issues may still involve vocational, ideological, and relational themes during adulthood as well as adolescence, but there may be somewhat dif-ferent balances of these concerns through adult life, as well as increasing concerns with existential issues.

Future research into ongoing identity development during adult life might focus on a number of interesting issues that have origins in Erik-son's work. Erikson's description of identity as a process of increasing differentiation during adulthood could be examined to determine more precisely what "differentiation" entails. One line of investigation might attempt to identify changing structural configurations of the self over adult life, as suggested by structural-developmental writers such as Robert Kegan (1982; 1994), Gil Noam (1988), and Jane Loevinger (1983). These researchers have examined developmentally different ways in which the individual comes to interpret and make sense of his or her life experiences over the course of the life span. All have proposed develop-mentally distinct ways in which the individual comes both to differentiate from and re-relate to that which is taken to be "other" over time.

Of value also would be further research into some of the specific identity revision and maintenance processes identified here. One might, for example, probe circumstances that help individuals to maintain a sense of identity continuity over time. Of particular interest might be the role that familiar objects play in this process. Rubenstein (1987) has found that valued possessions serve very important functions for those in their late adulthood years. Loss of spouse, friends, a social context, abili-ties, as well as a life era may give personal objects a special role in help-ing to signify and anchor one's sense of personal identity. Cram and Paton (1993) have found that valued possessions for the laterlife adult helps to bring alive memories of people, the creator of the object, and time or places, as well as giving one a sense of self-continuity. The question of how one maintains a sense of identity in the light of increasing memory loss is a further related area of investigation that might be productively explored.

The phenomenon of "tying up the package" might also be examined in relation to reminiscence research and the functions that reminiscence serves for identity maintenance in late adulthood. Robert Butler (1963) proposed that a life review is crucial in old age for optimal psychological functioning. Subsequent research on reminiscence has linked the ability to reflect over one's life with high scores on a measure of ego integrity and positive adaptation to stress (Taft and Nehrke, 1990; Lewis, 1971). Further research might fruitfully explore how concrete objects involved in "tying up the package" can facilitate or deter the process of reminiscence, and the role that reminiscence plays for identity maintenance in later adulthood.

Of crucial importance, also, are further researches into social contexts and the ways in which they facilitate or impede ongoing identity development during and beyond adolescence. While some studies of associations between social contexts or external life events and identity change have been undertaken and reviewed here, the interaction of social and historical contexts and complex life events with individual personality variables are badly needed. A start in this direction has been made by Stewart and Healy (1989). These investigators have proposed a model linking the influences of social events with individual personality development. Their model proposes that at any particular point in time, events impact individuals in a certain age cohort. Individuals of one cohort are involved in very different psychosocial tasks than those of other age cohorts. As a result, the same social or historical event is likely to affect individuals of different age cohorts in different ways. Future identity research should aim to understand more of these types of interactive processes, despite their complexities. Many issues await investigation in the area of ongoing identity development during adolescent and adult life that Erikson's groundbreaking efforts have inspired.

Conclusion

This chapter has considered the process of identity in formation. I began by presenting some of the varied meanings Erikson has bestowed upon the concept of ego identity and some of the vital functions that identity serves. Of identity's many ingredients, it is perhaps that sense of continuity and self-sameness that proves most vital to ongoing development over time. For Erikson, the tension between identity attainment and role confusion provides the impetus for identity's evolution throughout adolescent and adult life. While an initial resolution to the question of identity is generally made during late adolescence, identity considerations and revisions may reoccur over adult life.

James Marcia (1966, 1967) has elaborated on Erikson's understanding of the adolescent identity formation process. While Erikson had conceptualized resolution to the adolescent identity formation process as a position lying somewhere on a continuum between identity achievement and role confusion, Marcia conceptualized identity resolution in terms of one of four qualitatively distinct styles by which adolescents approach the identity formation task. Work based on both Erikson's and Marcia's identity frameworks point to the possibility of considerable scope for development during and beyond late adolescence. It is toward the exploration of such adult identity processes that the remainder of this chapter has turned.

In attempting to learn more about any such ongoing identity development (exploration and commitment) processes beyond adolescence, I undertook a small, qualitative investigation of identity through the eyes and life histories of fourteen later-life adults. This work pointed to a number of both identity revision and maintenance processes that individuals may employ to both modify and retain central identity elements over time. My suggestions for future research into ongoing identity development throughout adulthood focus on learning more about the ways in which "differentiation" takes place, continuity is maintained in the face of change, and social and historical circumstances shape and are shaped by identities in formation.

Identity formation and revision processes are not territories that one can enter lightly. These processes invariably involve great loss, great risk, as well as the potential for great gains. These processes may also produce developmental casualties along the way, as Erikson's clinical work with World War II veterans attests. While identity maintenance may be purchased at considerable cost, maintenance of some identity elements may be crucial to the optimal integration of new or revised fidelities. It lies in the hands of future identity researchers to identify both personal and social factors that may be associated with identity formation, identity revision, and maintenance processes during adult life and to ascertain their optimal balances over time.

References

Archer, S. L. "The Lower Age Boundaries of Identity Development," *Child Development* 53 (1982): 1551–56.

Berzonsky, M. D. "Self-identity: The Relationship between Process and Content," *Journal of Research in Personality* 28 (1994), no. 4: 453–460

Butler, R. "The Life Review: An Interpretation of Reminiscence in the Aged," *Psychiatry, Journal for the Study of Interpersonal Processes,* 26 (1963). Reprinted in B. L. Neugarten, ed., *Middle Age and Aging,* 486–496. Chicago: University of Chicago Press, 1968.

Campbell, E., G. R. Adams, and W. R. Dobson. "Familial Correlates of Identity Formation in Late Adolescence: A Study of the Predictive Utility of Connectedness and Individuality in Family Relations," *Journal of Youth and Adolescence* 13 (1984): 509–25.

Cram, F., and H. Paton. "Personal Possessions and Self-Identity: The Experiences of Elderly Women in Three Residential Settings," *Australian Journal on Ageing,* 12 (1993): 19–24.

Cramer, P. "Freshman to Senior Year: A Follow-Up Study of Identity, Narcissism, and Defense Mechanisms," *Journal of Research in Personality* 32 (1998): 156–72.

Erikson, E. H. "Identity and the Life Cycle," *Psychological Issues,* Monograph No. 1. New York: International Universities Press, 1959.

———. *Childhood and Society.* New York: W.W. Norton, 1963.

———. *Insight and Responsibility.* New York: W.W. Norton, 1964.

———. *Identity, Youth and Crisis.* New York: W.W. Norton, 1968.

———. *Life History and The Historical Moment.* New York: W.W. Norton, 1975.

Erikson, E. H., J. M. Erikson, and H. Kivnick. *Vital Involvement in Old Age.* New York: W.W. Norton, 1986.

Fitch, S. A., and G. R. Adams. "Ego Identity and Intimacy Status: Replication and Extension," *Developmental Psychology* 19 (1983): 839–45.

Grotevant, H. D., and C. R. Cooper. "Patterns of Interaction in Family Relationships and the Development of Identity Exploration in Adolescence," *Child Development* 56 (1985): 415–28.

Hoare, C. H. *Erikson on Adult Development: New Insights from Unpublished Papers.* Oxford: Oxford University Press, 2002.

Josselson, R. *Revising Herself: The Story of Women's Identity from College to Midlife.* New York: Oxford University Press, 1996.

Kegan, R. *The Evolving Self.* Cambridge. Mass.: Harvard University Press, 1982.

———. *In over Our Heads.* Cambridge, Mass.: Harvard University Press, 1994.

Kroger, J. "The Differentiation of 'Firm' and 'Developmental' Foreclosure Identity Statuses: A Longitudinal Study," *Journal of Research on Adolescence* 10 (1995): 317–37.

———. "Identity In Later Adulthood," *Identity: An International Journal of Theory and Research* 2 (2001): 81–99.

———. "Identity Development during Adolescence," in *The Blackwell Handbook Of Adolescence*, G. R. Adams and M. D. Berzonsky (eds.). Oxford: Blackwell Publishers Ltd., 2003.

———. and Green, K. (1996). "Events Associated with Identity Status Change," *Journal of Adolescence* 19, 477-490.

Kroger, J., and S. J. Haslett. "A Retrospective Study of Ego Identity Status Change from Adolescence through Middle Adulthood," *Social and Behavioral Sciences Documents* 17, ms. no. 2797 (1987).

———. "A Comparison of Ego Identity Status Transition Pathways and Change Rates across Five Identity Domains," *International Journal of Aging and Human Development* 32 (1991): 303-30.

Lewis, C. "Reminiscing and Self-Concept in Old Age," *Journal of Gerontology*, 26 (1971): 240-43.

Loevinger, J. "On Ego Development and the Structure of Personality," *Developmental Review* 3 (1983): 339-50.

Marcia, J. E. "Development And Validation of Ego Identity Status," *Journal of Personality and Social Psychology* 3 (1966): 551-58.

———. "Ego Identity Status: Relationship to Change in Self-Esteem, 'General Maladjustment,' and Authoritarianism," *Journal of Personality* 35 (1967): 18-31.

———. "Identity Six Years After: A Follow-Up Study," *Journal of Youth and Adolescence* 5 (1976): 145-50.

Marcia, J. E., A. S. Waterman, D. R. Matteson, S. L. Archer, and J. L. Orlofsky, *Ego Identity: A Handbook For Psychosocial Research*. New York: Springer-Verlag, 1993.

Noam, G. "The Self, Adult Development, and the Theory of Biography and Transformation," in D. K. Lapsley and F. C. Power (eds.), *Self, Ego, and Identity: Integrative Approaches*. New York: Springer-Verlag, 1988.

Perosa, L. M., S. L. Perosa, and H. P. Tam. "The Contribution of Family Structure and Differentiation to Identity Development in Females," *Journal of Youth and Adolescence* 25 (1996): 817-37.

Rubenstein, R. L. "The Significance of Personal Objects to Older People," *Journal of Aging Studies*, 1 (1987): 225-38.

Stevens, R. *Erik Erikson: An Introduction*. Oxford, England: Oxford University Press, 1983.

Stewart, A. J., and J. M. Healy. "Linking Individual Development And Social Changes," *American Psychologist* 44 (1989): 30-42.

Taft, L. B., and M. F. Nehrke, "Reminiscence, Life Review, and Ego Integrity in Nursing Home Residents," *International Journal of Aging and Human Development* 30 (1990): 189-96

Tesch, S. A., and K. A. Cameron, "Openness to Experience and Development of Adult Identity," *Journal of Personality* 55 (1987): 615-30.

Waterman, A. S., and J. A. Goldman. "A Longitudinal Study of Ego Identity Status Development at a Liberal Arts College," *Journal of Youth and Adolescence* 5 (1976): 361-69.

Waterman, A. S., P. S. Geary, and C. K. Waterman. "Longitudinal Study of Changes in Ego Identity Status from the Freshman to the Senior Year at College," *Developmental Psychology* 10 (1974): 387-92.

Willemsen E. W., and K. K. Waterman. "Ego Identity Status and Family Environment: A Correlational Study," *Psychological Reports* 69 (1991): 1203-12.

Chapter Six

Identity and Choice

Kristen Renwick Monroe

Erik Erikson was one of those rare individuals who inspires us as both scholars and as human beings, and I want to try to honor this dual contribution by asking what a study of identity—the topic with which Erikson is perhaps most closely associated—can tell us about broader issues of concern to us as human beings, as well as scholars. Essentially, the chapter presented here considers the tremendous power of identity to shape our most basic social behavior. It focuses on identity's ability to constrain critical political and moral choice and explores the implications of this constraint for political and social theory.

The chapter draws on my research, taken as a whole since 1988, but I will concentrate my remarks on what I have learned from my studies of four related topics: altruism, moral choice during the Holocaust, ethnic violence in the contemporary Middle East, and theoretical work in social and political theory. Let me first summarize the empirical work on which I base my general comments, and then suggest what a study of identity tells us about broader issues of concern to political psychologists. [1]

Empirical Foundation

Altruism

Beginning in 1988, I have been fortunate to spend time with a number of different altruists, from philanthropists and rescuers of Jews to recipients of the Carnegie Hero award. My in-depth interviews with these altruists, presented in a series of publication (1991, 2002) suggested it was altruists' identities and, more particularly, their perceptions of themselves in relation to others, that worked to constrain and shape the choices they found available, not just morally but empirically. I later examined rescuers more carefully, and contrasted their behavior with the traditional literature on moral choice (2002). This analysis suggested that the most frequently offered explanations for moral choice—reason or religion—were not what led rescuers to risk their lives to save Jews. Instead, it was their sense that "we are all human beings" and that protecting human life and well-being constitutes the essence of morality. Both of these projects led me to identity as an explanation for, or at least a critical constraining influence on, some of our most basic political and ethical acts.

The Holocaust: A Study in Contrasts

The second set of research also considers the Holocaust but moved beyond rescuers to include interviews with bystanders, Nazi sympathizers and even a few Nazis (1994a, 2001b). In doing so, I wanted to inquire further about the importance of identity to ask whether identity constrained choice for all individuals, or just for the morally exemplary. This comparative analysis was extremely useful in suggesting the psychological process through which identity works to constrain choice. This process involved distinct patterns of cognitive classification or categorization, and a relational form of perspective. What was interesting to me is that while identity might be conceptualized as character—a biological, socially constructed and a cognitive phenomenon—the process through which identity appears to exert its ethical and political influence was cognitive.

Genocide and Ethnic Violence: Perpetrators

In joint work with Lina Kreidie (Kreidie and Monroe 2002a, 2002b), I inquired about the psychological dimension of ethnic conflict. Kreidie's unusual access to perpetrators of communal violence from 1975 to 1989 during the Lebanese civil war gave us the opportunity to interview five perpetrators of atrocities. Our interviews focused on trying to understand how identity constrains choice and works to turn ordinary people toward ethnic violence. Although only a pilot project, the interviews present striking evidence that identity constrains choice for all individuals, regardless of their particular ideology, ethnicity, or socioeconomic demographic background. Our findings challenge the rationalist approaches of realistic conflict theory and rational choice, contradict the institutional claims of consociational democracy, and suggest the tremendous political power of identity and perceptions of self in relation to others.

Identity and Social and Political Theory

As an empirical political theorist, I am interested in the implications of empirical work for social and political theory. My studies of identity have led me to argue (1994b, 2001a) that rational choice theory rests on assumptions concerning human nature that are too narrow; as a theoretical framework, rational choice thus will have limited value in explaining the full range of sociopolitical human behavior. I believe rational choice theory can be subsumed by a theory about identity. Such an identity theory should include that aspect of identity in which there is a powerful human drive toward self-interest and rational calculus; but it also needs to allow for innate needs for human connection and focus on how our perceptions of our identities and our relationships to others shift over time and in response to external stimuli and situational factors.

Taken as a whole, these empirical findings raise several important questions of interest to both political psychologists and political theorists. What is the moral psychology, and what is the psychological process through which identity and perspective influence social, political, and ethical action? What part of behavior can we explain through identity and a sense of self in relation to others? Can we actually develop a political theory that relies on identity and how we classify and categorize ourselves in relation to others? And finally, can this kind of analysis of identity help us rethink our most basic theories of human political action by focusing attention on the extent to which our choices result from our fundamental sense of what it means to be human?

Implications of Studying Identity

Let me now turn to a few general thoughts about what these empirical findings suggest we can learn from a study of identity. More precisely, perhaps, let me ask what we can learn if we try to think about these issues as Erikson might have done. Doing so leads me to six different areas of potential insight.

Identity as a Constraint on Moral Action

All the interviews I conducted—with individuals as diverse as entrepreneurs and altruists, rescuers and Nazis—yield insight into issues of ethics and morality and show us that identity constrains moral choice. They reveal both the complexity and the multiplicity of forces driving the moral life. If we consider just the moral exemplars—our rescuers of Jews, for example—we find many different factors at work: duty, outrage, religion, an innate moral sense, socialization, role modeling and mentors, even a desire to show off. While all of these factors are frequently related to moral motivation, however, the many times when such factors are absent makes it prudent to conclude that these factors constitute a facilitating but not necessarily an essential impetus toward doing good. What is perhaps more striking, as we sort through the myriad possible forces driving morality, is one startling omission: the lack of choice. Instead of the agonistic choice that lies at the heart of traditional explanations for much of ethics, we find identity. This is not to discount the importance of other influences on the moral life; it merely suggests the tremendous and too frequently overlooked role played by identity and perspective in triggering our actions. At least for the people I interviewed, character counted more than the influences traditionally said to provide the impetus behind moral action, and emotions and feelings trumped the cool and impartial calculus of reason.

Integration of Moral Values into One's Sense of Identity

For the morally commendable, the ethical values of human well-being and the sanctity of life had become so intricately integrated into their basic sense of who they were that their commitment to these values shaped the central core of their identities. It thus became unthinkable for altruists intentionally to engage in behavior that would contradict the essence of their identity.[2] The incorporation of these values into the altruist's sense of self effectively created boundaries in their self-image that limited and foreclosed any debate about transgressing these values. Because these particular moral values—human well-being and the sanctity of life—were so integrated into the altruist's core identity, these commitments took on a quality of unquestioning quasi-finality.

This phenomenon is evident in the testimony of one of the Resistance leaders, a Dutchman named John Weidner, who was on the Gestapo's most-wanted list and who was captured and escaped five times. When asked about the torture to which he was subjected, and why he never broke under these interrogations, John said he never even considered the question of whether he would reveal information under torture. The extent to which certain values had become integrated into the rescuers' identities is further illustrated by the extent to which rescuers performed similar altruistic acts both before and after World War II. It is evident in the degree to which rescuers' acts were not marked by any of the inner battles or hesitations we frequently associate with agonistic moral choices. And the integration is evident in the lack of choice and the absence of calculation of risks, costs, and benefits.[3]

An analogous phenomenon occurred for nonrescuers. The perpetrators interviewed for my research on the Holocaust and for the Kreidie-Monroe analysis of ethnic violence in the contemporary Middle East also illustrated the importance of both identity and the integration of values into one's sense of self. Moreover, whereas the particular values differed slightly, the differences were not as great as one might hypothesize. Perpetrators tended to be more particularistic than universal in their ethics, speaking of ethics in terms that privilege the tribe, group, nation, or ethnicity as the limit of legitimate moral concern, while rescuers tended to use the language of universalist ethics based on the idea of human rights. But both groups of individuals had what an objective observer might conclude were high moral values.

Perceptions and the Relational Aspect of Identity's Influence

It did not appear to be specific values or even—at one level—perceptions of self that were key, however, since both groups of people might use the same language, even the same phrases to describe themselves. Indeed, Florentine (a totally unrepentant Nazi, widow of one of the top Dutch Nazis, and sister to the head of the Dutch SS) described her husband was an "idealist" who refused to be spirited to South America after the war, along with other top Nazis, and instead stayed in Holland "in order to tell the truth" about what had happened. What *was* different was Florentine's perception of herself and her sense of ontological security. Florentine clearly saw herself, and others in her tribe, as being threatened by the Jews, the gypsies, the Social Democrats, etc. This dimension of her self-perception had important implications for Florentine's categorization schema. To best understand Florentine's cognitive framework, think of your attitude toward a cockroach you find in your house. You have no compunction in killing the cockroach because you see it as being in a category that is both subhuman and potentially harmful to you. This is the way Florentine's categorization system operated. As bizarre as it seemed, I am prepared to believe Florentine genuinely sees herself as someone who was the innocent party during World War II, someone who had to defend herself against forces that would destroy the health of the good Dutch body politic.[4]

In this regard, the sense of one's self in relation to other people seemed the critical factor for both perpetrators and for the rescuers I interviewed. Moreover, a critical aspect of this sense seemed to center on perceptions.[5] I conclude, then, that it is not just identity but also the relationship between the actor and "the other" that is paramount. Because the rescuers saw themselves as people strongly committed to certain moral principles, because they refused to characterize Jews in any category other than the one to which all human beings belong, and because they felt all human beings were entitled to decent treatment merely by virtue of being human, the rescuers genuinely could not "see" any other option than to help their fellow human beings. To do otherwise was unimaginable.[6] Because Florentine could not see the humanity in those she persecuted, because she saw them as subhuman, and because she believed they would hurt her if possible, she felt no guilt for her actions. Even today, she insists Hitler was a great man, someone she compared to Christ and Gandhi.

This categorization process is one aspect of the moral psychology—as a general phenomenon—that we need to explore more fully in future work.

The Moral Psychology

If we examine only the positive aspect of the moral psychology, i.e., the psychological process that leads us to what we think of as ethically *commendable* actions, then the rescuers prove most instructive. Their stories suggest a more general process by which universal and possibly innate human needs for consistency[7] and self-esteem[8] provide a foundation for moral action that is not based on religion, reason, or externally imposed rules or laws. I gained some insight into how the moral psychology operates by listening to rescuers and can, as a result, suggest something like the following process in which how we categorize and classify others influences our treatment of them.

Each of us wants to be treated well. Once we recognize that other people have a similar need, we are led to extend these universal rights of entitlement reciprocally, treating others as we ourselves wish to be treated. The moral psychology is reminiscent of tenets found in both religious teachings (e.g., Christianity's Golden Rule) and philosophical systems of ethics (e.g., Kant's categorical imperative). Insofar as this ethical reciprocity is a fundamental correlate of the human capacity for intersubjective communication and the psychological need to distinguish boundaries via categorization, however, such an ethical reciprocity appears more basic than an intellectualized sense of duty or religious doctrine. Indeed, the power of such religious or philosophical admonitions actually may emanate from their resonance with the basic moral psychology. It is possible that the moral psychology originates in a kind of innate moral sense, born into all people, which then develops differentially in phenotypic fashion, depending on external forces in the environment.[9] While this theoretical conclusion is speculative, and must await further empirical examination, my initial analysis (2001b) of behavior of individuals at all parts of the moral spectrum provides further insight into the role of cognitive classification and categorization in turning us toward good or bad in our treatment of others.

Cognitive Classification and Categorization

I assume identity is composed of some combination of biologically inherited predispositions, cognitive processes, and social construction via cultural influences, including socialization and treatment from others. The process we call social construction is how we introduce the importance of others, and psychology as a discipline has already devoted a fair bit of attention to this topic. Our challenge now is to work with cognitive scientists to better understand the cognitive processes at work here, especially to focus on the ethical implications of how we see ourselves, how we process information, and how we prepare cognitive scenarios to help us avoid moral dilemmas. My empirical work suggests there may be great intellectual traction in doing so. For example, one rescuer—a Czech in the Resistance—told of creating a scenario in advance that would help him avoid revealing information were he to be captured and tortured.[10] Nowhere was the ethical consequences of categorization and classification of other people more obvious than in my comparative analysis of rescuers, bystanders, and perpetrators; this finding makes me suspect that attempts at healing and reconciliation after violent conflicts will have to address this cognitive conceptualization if they are to be successful.

Importance of Identity for Social and Political Theory: The Need to Focus on Human Flourishing, Not Individual Self-Interest or Community

The influence from identity is complex and subtle but extensive, and should not be ignored by social and political theorists. Consider the rescuers as an example. The rescuers show us an alternative way of viewing one's self. On this dimension, their cognitive frameworks do not fit into the categories currently in vogue in academic circles, in which analysts assume a dichotomous view of our relationship to others. This dichotomy has appeared in many forms at different points in time[11] but essentially juxtaposes the individual with the group or community, and poses a tension between following individual self-interest versus caring for others. The rescuers suggest this tension may be more an artificial—albeit analytically useful—construct than it is an actual part of the human psychology.

Thinking about the theoretical implications of identity focused me on three questions that had not occurred to me before. How do we understand what I came to think of as human connection? How does human connection in turn relate to human flourishing? And why is this important for social theory? The psychological literature tells us how basic and fundamental is our need for recognition and acknowledgment. This literature suggests we are not merely atomistic individuals, and that our need for others is more than our need for their cooperation in our own individualistic enterprises or even for help in ensuring individual survival. It is instead a fundamental part of our human nature to crave acceptance, validation, and affirmation from others. We can find self-esteem and self-respect only when others help us claim it.[12] The challenge is to figure out how this connection is made and with whom.

There is much further evidence, from a variety of sources, that human connection is necessary for human flourishing.[13] Human connection is more than merely affirming shared values. Human connection means finding others with whom one shares not just values but a common frame of reference, a common way of seeing the world. Since human connection is not a standard behavioral concept—indeed, it may sound like psychobabble to a hard-nosed experimentalist—let me try to make it more precise. In doing so, perhaps it is not surprising that one of the most faithful capturing of what I am trying to express comes from a description of the loss of a mother.

> Old friends rallied to give him [Isaiah Berlin] comfort. He confessed to Herbert Hart and to Jean Floud that he felt as if the roof of his life had blown off. The word that kept recurring to him was *Zerrissenheit*. It meant being torn to pieces. For a week or so he was in deep mourning, weighing his loss and looking back over the terrain he had traveled in her company. He suddenly felt horribly alone. Life seemed to have lost its story-line and his own existence seemed accidental. The link to the most intimate of his loyalties had been snapped. She had been the real unacknowledged source of his Herderian beliefs —in Jewishness, in belonging, in the very necessity of having roots. She had given him that existential certainty, that confidence in his own judgment, which had allowed him to *live* his life and not merely inhabit it, as his father had done. With her death, he told a friend, the pillars that held up his life had cracked; while the cracks would soon be covered over with makeshift plaster, the pillars would never be as solid again. (Ignatieff, 1998, 272)

Developmental psychologists and psychoanalysts discuss something similar to this as attachment theory. This theory suggests a child must form deep bonds with another person—most frequently, in contemporary Western society these are with the mother—in order to develop the sense of self necessary to then achieve autonomy, and to form bonds with others. A discussion of these bonds, which form a critical part of what it means to be a human being and whose origins, I would argue, are rooted deep within our human nature as basic drives, cannot be void of content. The values of others, the way others see and make sense of the world, must validate and affirm our own view.

This connection is what culture often supplies to people, a sense of sharing not just values but a common, understandable, and positively valenced way of looking at the world. Groups provide this sense for many of us. The nature of the group can vary, from the ethnic-religious groups of the perpetrators examined in the Kreidie-Monroe study to self-help groups like Alcoholics Anonymous, that help reconnect us to that small child who got lost in the dysfunction of our lives. Too often, discussion of community values and communitarian organizations fails to address the nature of the group. Groups can have power, even if the group is a destructive, evil group, such as the Nazis; indeed, my interviews with perpetrators forced me to remember that the Nazis supplied a critical—if warped—sense of connection for many in the Third Reich who felt lost, beaten, and alone. Such is the power of groups and of culture, to provide human connection.

In constructing our social and political theories, we should not treat this human connection as something in lieu of self-interest in the traditional economic sense of protecting oneself against the harsh world. But to forge human connection, one must find the strength to be vulnerable, to be open to others, even if this means we can be hurt. We cannot always be protected and still have human connection. A person therefore must relinquish some of the protection of self-interest as Hobbes conceived of it, in order to have the human connection that is that part of self-interest necessary for human flourishing.

Humanistic Implications of Work on Identity

A discussion of human connection returns me to a consideration of Erikson's more humanistic contributions, and I would like to conclude by speaking about the questions my empirical work raised about our ties to others and what we need to flourish as individuals.[14] In doing so, I attempt to honor Erikson's concern that we engage not only as scholars but also as individuals involved in a world that is often troubling and one in which our scholarship should inform and enrich the way we conduct and compose our own lives.

I turn here to my rescuers. For the rescuers, any "choice" to save Jews was described as part of a broader decision concerning the kind of person one was. Rescuers' insistence on the ordinary aspect of their acts suggests rescue activities were not considered agonistic moral choices so much as the natural steps on a path chosen by a prior molding as a certain kind of human being. To have turned away from the Jews would have meant turning away from one's self. By showing us this, the rescuers remind us how important our ties with others are in preserving our own identities.[15] As one rescuer said, "I think that we all have memories of times that we should have done something and we didn't. And it gets in your way during the rest of your life."[16]

Identity constrains action, but acts, in turn, shape and chisel at one's identity as we construct a life. It is this insight that offers us a different way of seeing things. By providing us a close, personal view of this moral perspective, the rescuers reveal an alternative way to view the self, one that is more basic in linking one's treatment of others to one's sense of self-worth. For the rescuers, identity and perceptions were critical factors in their treatment of Jews. It was the rescuers' sense of human connection that caused them to risk their lives for other human beings. But this human connection also provided rescuers with something essential for their own well-being.

To understand moral choice during the Holocaust, we have to enter those dark places of our own souls, places we avoid much of the time. In part, this is because the rescuers' stories take us to a terrible time in history, one that is deeply disturbing for most of us to read about. But perhaps an equally unsettling aspect of these stories is the extent to which examining the lives of rescuers forces us to ask troubling questions about our own lives.

World War II was a period when people could not avoid difficult questions. They had to confront the unimaginable. It was a time when people had to be their big selves. They could not easily avoid issues of character. But character did not always predict behavior. Good people were not always the ones who rose to the occasion, and scoundrels sometimes did. (Witness the moral failure of Pope Pius XII[17] and the commendable rescue activities of Oskar Schindler.)

The rescuers met the challenge. When tested, they showed themselves to be people who were morally exemplary. Indeed, we still find ourselves filled with awe and admiration for them. But—perhaps more importantly—they are exemplars who are easy to love. They have foibles, eccentricities, failed marriages, bumpy relations with their children. Their very humanness makes them more endearing, more accessible, more like us. And therein lies both their value and their ability to disturb our moral composure.

One incident with a German woman named Margot sticks out in my mind. Margot was quite wealthy—her father was head of General Motors for Western Europe—and Margot left Germany shortly after Hitler took power, as a protest against Nazi policies. She moved to Holland with her husband and two small children and later worked in the Resistance, where she rescued both Jews and Allied airmen. After the war she came to California and I met her in 1988, while conducting my study of altruism. We became close over the years and on one of my visits Margot showed me a book manuscript she had written about her beloved fiancé, Alfred, murdered by the Nazis because of Margot. Margot wrote the book in the third person, using a pseudonym, and allowed it to be copyrighted but not published. Margot said she wanted to give me the book but couldn't, because of this copyright, but that it was all right to use the material from it in my own work.

I interpret Margot's unpublished book as her attempt to deal with the powerful emotions left from the war. I was struck by Margot's touching ambivalence about revealing writing that so fully captures who she is and how she thinks. The fact that Margot wrote the book in the third person, and was so tentative about sharing it with me. Her phrase as she showed me the manuscript: "I'd like you to have it but I can't give it away." All these indicators are subtle and I may be reading too much into them, but they seem evidence of how deeply felt is Margot's need for connectedness and the powerful force this bond, established with Alfred, still holds for Margot, fifty years after his death. As painful as it was to lose this relationship, Margot's book also suggests the importance of human connection in enabling a decent and sensitive woman to hold on to her sanity, to maintain a sense of self that is wounded but not destroyed by the horrors of war.[18]

The introduction to Margot's book seems to represent Margot's attempt to understand or at least to reflect upon the meaning of her life:

> It has been said many times that one might be able to relive one's past. I don't believe this. However, if it were at all possible, I hear people say that they would return to Mother Earth as the very same person they are now. But they would change most of the events and occurrences that happened in their lives. They swore that they would not repeat the mistakes they had made but would instead alter the flow of happenings and thus reconstruct the course of history. Impossible. I believe in all the wonderful and tragic moments and would never change one instant in my life, even if I could. The trials, errors, heartaches, delights and ecstasies are part of life itself. The deep love of two beings melted into one is the ultimate fulfillment. The hardships that teach understanding form the character within one's self. The injustices against the innocent are the experience and knowledge of grim reality. Above all, there is the ability to help alleviate the pain of fellow human beings. This I believe is the ultimate goal of our short existence on this earth.

This passage eloquently communicates the subtle but powerful aspect of human connection in providing not just friendship and the pleasures of sociability—valuable as these are—but also a fundamental human need to find meaning in life and to discover a sense of ourselves through others. It captures the power of human connection in providing the rescuers not only with the ability to save others but also with the awareness that their recognition of another's humanity was part of what gave meaning to their own lives.

Margot's moving expression of the value of human connection was not unique. I experienced similar exchanges with other rescuers. A Polish rescuer (Irene) told about saving Jews in the home of a German major. When Irene was caught, the major forced Irene to become his mistress in exchange for his silence. At the end of our interviews, I asked Irene about the people she had saved, and whether she knew what had happened to some of the other people she had known during the war. Had Irene been able to make sense of all these events, I wondered. Was she able to find any meaning in what had happened to her?

> *Q. What I'm hearing you say is that it's very difficult to maintain the kind of human communication during a war. That because of the situation, individuals are forced to choose up sides of one kind. But that you and the people you associated with were able to reach across those barriers and find some kind of human communication, a bond. The Major. Ida and her little boy. A major who could have turned you all in, who did something in some ways which was very unfair to you, but which was motivated out of love and affection.*
>
> A. Yes, because it was. I mean he did really love me. I cannot say that he was brutal. He was not beating me or anything. He was very direct, very allowing, expressing himself. He would say, "Irene, is that so bad? I keep your secret. I will help you. And you give old man the last joy in his life."
>
> Then after the war, the people that he had helped, in turn helped him, and he becomes a grandfather to the boy [Ida's son].
>
> You see! It is such a story I wanted to tell. That there are bad and good people. And I am not trying to put hate on any particular group. The time is for us to reach to each other. That's the only way we can be safe, even now.

Human connection was the key. Their sense of being connected to the Jews through bonds of a common humanity was what drove the rescuers to do the impossible, to save people from the clutches of an all-powerful state. The rescuers gave, gave generously and with no thought of repayment, to be sure. But this spontaneous giving had an unexpected consequence. Caring for others helped *them* remain connected, not just to others but to themselves. The fact that these rescuers—very human people all, not plaster saints—were able to remain aware of these bonds, even in the midst of unrelenting societal and political pressure to ignore such attachments, shows us both the power and the value of a different way of seeing the world.[19] This way is not the simple calculus of self-interest we find in economics or evolutionary biology, in the cost-benefit analysis of decision-making theory or the rational choice analysis found throughout much of contemporary social science. Nor is it the communitarian's world of groups, in which the mental image of "us versus them" can too easily turn "different from" into "better than," as it did for the Nazis.[20]

Resistance to genocide is not just an affirmation of universalism in which every human being is entitled to rights and equal treatment by virtue of being born human. It is more than simply seeing the humanity in the Jews, more than seeing the bonds that connect us. It is also a cherishing, a celebration of all the differences—individual and group—that allow for human flourishing, set firmly within the context of universal worth. This is what the rescuers protected for all of us when they resisted genocide, prejudice, and ethnic violence. Their very ordinariness, their very humanness, encourages us to look deep within our own souls and ask if we, too, do not possess this possibility.

I believe Erik Erikson—born of a Jewish mother and a father he did not know, who created his own name, much as he created the contemporary scholarly field of identity to weave together the personal and the political, and someone who fought for human freedom his entire life—would encourage us in this enterprise.

Notes

1. Parts of this chapter appear in *The Hand of Compassion: Portraits of Moral Choice during the Holocaust* (Princeton University Press, Princeton, NJ, 2004). We are grateful to Princeton University Press for their permission to include excerpts in this volume. These findings reject the kind of reflective equilibrium prevalent in contractarian approaches to morality (Rawls, 1971) or in rational choice theory.

2. See Frankfurt, 1988, for an excellent discussion of identity, moral character, and will.

3. All of this is in line with the kinds of characteristics that Frankfurt argues we find in the type of will in which we find wholehearted commitment to moral values and desires. Frankfurt notes that morality is only one of many possible values that an individual may care deeply about and structure his/her will around, a point I find extremely important and which I pursue empirically in a forthcoming volume on Nazis and bystanders, as well as rescuers.

4. Lerner (1992) found this same phenomenon among German health officials during World War II.

5. Blasi's empirical work underlines the importance of integration. His recent theoretical work (2002) stresses the importance of perceptions. See Blasi, chapter 3, 28.

6. The importance of the moral imagination—a cognitive phenomenon—is one topic I hope will be explored more fully in future work.

7. As utilized by psychologists, self-consistency usually refers to some combination of both behavioral and trait consistency and the many different varieties of logical and cognitive consistency, including coherence among representations of the self. These conceptualizations underlie the basic research on cognitive dissonance (Festinger, 1957), as well as the work on personality integration (Blasi, 1988).

8. I would hypothesize that the relationship between consistency and self-esteem is linked to the extent to which a rescuer's commitments and values are such that the central or core self is constructed around them. We might think of these as the values or ideals that truly matter to a person and which provide a sense of meaning in the person's life. Frankfurt argues that these core values are so much a part of one's self that betraying them constitutes the same thing as betraying one's soul. See Frankfurt, 1988.

9. The best recent psychological work on moral psychology is Blasi (1980, 1988, 1995, 2002). In 2002, chapter 3, Blasi traces the development of moral character as an approach within psychology. Blasi notes that behaviorism tended to reduce personality to a conglomerate of habits; only after Piaget, did the American psychological community begin to understand the importance of cognition for morality. Kohlberg's work expanded on Piaget's cognitive developmental approach in such a powerful fashion that work on moral psychology is only now understanding the limitations of the cognitive developmental approach.

Blasi's most recent work reintroduces the concept of moral character, but does so in a manner that draws on both philosophical discussions, especially those of virtue ethics, and the most recent, rigorous psychological work. Blasi (2002, 4) argues that moral character involves predispositions, which Blasi defines as relatively stable and general personality characteristics. Blasi then defines these personality characteristics in terms of their relation to action, an approach that differentiates his view from those of the cognitive-develop mentalists. Finally, Blasi assumes that intentions and motives count in speaking of moral character, and that there must be some minimal grasp of what morality is and involves.

10. Blasi, 2002, noted a similar phenomenon.

11. In 1887, Ferdinand Tönnies (1925) argued for two basic forms of human association, reflecting different beliefs about the nature of the self and social relationships: *Gemeinschaft* and *Gesellschaft* worldviews. Gemeinschaft (translated as community) refers to close, holistic social relationships of family and kin groups in preindustrial communities. Individuals cannot be taken out of the context of a society and are born with obligations, ties, and identities as part of that community. People with this worldview have a "consciousness of belonging together and the affirmation of the condition of mutual dependence" (Tönnies, 1925, 69), and a sense of moral worth is attached to these close community ties. In contrast, we find the Gesellschaft worldview, translated as association or society and characterized as postindustrial, urban, and modern. This Gesellschaft worldview conceptualizes the self as an individual independent of others, who

acts rationally, efficiently, and instrumentally to further voluntarily chosen goals. Social ties are understood to be based on a union of rational wills, with membership sustained by some instrumental goal or definite end. Barry (1970) argues that we find a similar distinction between traditional sociologists and economists. With the incursion of rational choice analysis into sociology, this distinction has broken down somewhat, but we find a similar conceptual divide in the debates between liberals and rational actor theorists versus communitarians.

12. This help need not occur at the moment of action, and can extend to our early childhood days, when our early sense of self is established through our interactions with others.

13. Aristotle, of course, suggested that man is a social being. Contemporary psychology provides ample evidence in a wide variety of fields, from personality and developmental to abnormal psychology, that people need others to reflect, validate, and affirm their sense of self, that most basic sense of who we are.

14. To the extent to which we emphasize the social side of the self, we need to ask about the extent to which we are trapped within that society. What if our genetic predispositions make us unhappy in the society into which we are born? Make us gravitate toward values at odds with the basic values in our community? Will we become the moral analogues of left-handed children being forced to use our right hands?

One implication of the atomistic conception of individuals is universalism since if what makes us distinct, what makes us what we are, is our ability to reason, and if all humans have this basic ability, then we move toward universalism. And if what makes us individuals is the idea of reason, then isn't every reasoning being equal? We might think of this equivalence and equality as the good aspect of universalism. A more pernicious aspect of universalism comes if we assume every individual should think in a particular manner of abstract reasoning, such as that which Descartes admired, and we then privilege individuals and cultures that excel at this particular form, as happens in many disciplines within academics.

Another implication of this dichotomy concerns human connection. If as Aristotle suggests, every person is a social being, then people in every culture want to be bound together, not just into families but into larger social groups and even polities; hence, much of our identity becomes group identity or social identity. Indeed, our self will not be satisfied unless it is nested in a rich set of relations with others. This need for others is a part of our basic identity, a reflection of our need to find out and to know who we are which can be satisfied only in the reflection of others. We see ourselves reflected in the eyes of others.

But which others? What if the people around us do not see us as we wish to be seen? As we genuinely feel we are? Are we merely the social construction of others? Do we have no free will? And what happens to moral responsibility if identity is not our own creation? These are difficult questions for which I have no answers.

15. The tension between caring for others and the loss one feels from them once they are taken from us is poignantly expressed in the writings of Holocaust survivors, such as Primo Levi (1961) and Elie Wiesel (1960, 1992), the filmed testimonies with survivors (Langer, 1991) and films (*Shadows* or *Sophie's Choice*).

16. Marion, interview for Carol Rittener and Sandra Myers, *The Courage to Care*. New York: New York University Press, 1986.

17. There are several excellent recent books on the controversial activities of the Catholic popes during the Holocaust. See inter alia Zuccotti, 2000.

18. Langer's (1991) analysis of the oral testimonies of concentration camp survivors focuses on the contradictory value of forgetting painful memories. For some survivors, forgetting the past was necessary in order to survive. For others, remembering the past was a survival mechanism. I would interpret this phenomenon not as a contradiction but rather as an indicator of the force of the human mind, which does not deal with difficult issues until the person is able to do so. I might further argue that it was, at least in part, the rescuers' ability to retain these ties that kept them from experiencing the psychic discontinuities that Langer finds among survivors. Indeed, some of the testimonies Langer cites suggest the importance of human attachment for camp inmates. (In one particularly poignant story, a survivor tells of being on a train with another girl, a girl who finds and cares for a baby while en route to camp. Because the girl refuses to leave the baby, she is sent to die with the baby. The woman relating the story, years later, seems to envy this girl, who found something to love and care for, even if the attachment meant her death.) Wiesel (1960, 1992) and Levi (1961) also allude to this phenomenon.

19. I have elsewhere (1996) referred to this as the altruistic perspective.

20. See Monroe, 1995b, 2001b for a discussion of the importance of categorization for genocide, prejudice, and ethnic violence. Perhaps the most important question is what makes some human beings resist genocide while others ignore, support, or commit it.

References

Barry, B. *Economists, Sociologists and Democracy*. Chicago: University of Chicago Press, 1970.

Blasi, A. "Bridging Moral Cognition and Moral Action: A Critical Review of the Literature," *Psychological Bulletin* 88 (1980): 1–45.

———. "Identity and Development of the Self," in *Self, Ego, and Identity: Integrative Approaches*, D. K. Lapsley and F. C. Power (eds.). New York: Springer-Verlag, 1988.

———. "The Development of Identity: Some Implications for Moral Functioning," in *The Moral Self*, G. G. Noam and T. E. Wren (eds.). Cambridge, MA: MIT Press, 1993.

———. "A Moral Understanding and the Moral Personality: The Process of Moral Integration," in *Moral Development: An Introduction*, W. M. Kurtines and J. L. Gewirtz (eds.). Boston: Allyn Bacon, 1995.

———.Untitled book manuscript, 2002, chapter 3.

Festinger, L.. *A Theory of Cognitive Dissonance*. Stanford, CA: Stanford University Press, 1957.

Festinger, L., and E. Aronson. "The Arousal and Reduction of Dissonance in Social Contexts," in *Group Dynamics*, D. Cartwright and A. Zander (eds.). Evanston, IL: Row, Peterson, 1960.

Festinger, L., H. W. Riecken, and S. Schachter. *When Prophesy Fails.* Minneapolis: University of Minnesota Press, 1957.

Frankfurt, H. *Importance of What We Care About.* Cambridge, MA: Harvard University Press, 1988.

Ignatieff, M. *Isaiah Berlin: A Life.* New York, NY: Metropolitan Books, 1998.

Kreidie, L. H., and K. R. Monroe. "The Psychological Dimension of Ethnic Conflict: How Identity Constrained Choice and Worked to Turn Ordinary People into Perpetrators of Ethnic Violence during the Lebanese Civil War," *International Journal of Politics, Culture and Society.* 16, no. 1 (Fall, 2002a): 5–36.

————."Psychological Boundaries and Ethnic Conflict: How Identity Constrained Choice and Worked to Turn Ordinary People into Perpetrators of Ethnic Violence during the Lebanese Civil War," *International Journal Of Politics, Culture And Society*, 16, no. 1 (Fall 2002b) 5-36.

————. "The Perspectives of Islamic Fundamentalists and the Limits of Rational Choice Theory." *Political Psychology* 18, no. 1 (1997): 19–43.

Langer, L. *Holocaust Testimonies.* New Haven, CT: Yale University Press, 1991.

Lerner, R. *Final Solutions: Biology, Prejudice, and Genocide.* University Park: Penn State University Press, 1992.

Levi, P. *Survival in Auschwitz: The Nazi Assault on Humanity.* Trans. Stuart Woolf. New York, NY: Collier-Macmillan, 1961.

Monroe, Kristen. "How Identity and Perspective Constrain Moral Choice," *International Political Science Review* 24, No. 4 (2003) 405-25.

————. " Identity and Moral Choice: The Moral Psychology and the Humane Response to Ethnic Violence," paper presented at the annual meetings of the International Society of Political Psychology, Berlin, 2002. Overview of a book manuscript, forthcoming.

————. "Paradigm Shift: From Rational Choice to Perspective." *The International Political Science Review.* 22, no. 2 (April 2001a): 151–172.

————. "Moral Action and a Sense of Self: The Importance of Categorization for Moral Action," *The American Journal of Political Science* 45, no. 3 (July 2001b): 491–507.

————. "The Perspectives of Islamic Fundamentalists and the Limits of Rational Choice Theory." *Political Psychology* 18, 1 (1997): 19-43. Coauthored with Lina Haddad Kreidie.

————. *The Heart of Altruism: Perceptions of a Common Humanity.* Princeton, NJ: Princeton University Press, 1996.

————. "Psychology and Rational Actor Theory." Editor's introduction to a special issue of *Political Psychology* 16, 1 (March 1995a): 1- 42.

————. "The Psychology of Genocide: A Review of the Literature." *Ethics and International Affairs* 9 (1995b) 215–239.

————. "'But What Else Could I Do?' A Cognitive-Perceptual Theory of Ethical Political Behavior," *Political Psychology* 16, no. 1 (1994a): 1–22.

————. "A Fat Lady in a Corset: Altruism and Social Theory." *The American Journal of Political Science* 38, no. 4 (1994b): 861–893.

————. "John Donne's People: Explaining Differences between Rational Actors and Altruists through Cognitive Frameworks," *The Journal of Politics* 53, no. 2 (1991): 394–433.

94 *Monroe*

———. "Altruism and the Theory of Rational Action: An Analysis of Rescuers of Jews in Nazi-Europe," *Ethics* 101 (1990): 103-122.

Rawls, J. *A Theory of Justice.* Cambridge, MA: Harvard University Press, 1971.

Tönnies, F. *Community and Association / Gemeinschaft und Gesellschaft.* Trans. Charles P. Loomis. East Lansing, MI: Michigan State University Press, 1925/1957.

Wiesel, E. *Night.* New York: Bantam, 1960.

———. *The Forgotten.* New York: Summit, 1992.

Zuccotti, S. *Under His Very Window: The Vatican and the Holocaust in Italy.* New Haven, CT: Yale University Press, 2000.

Part Three

The Future

Chapter Seven

What Should Democracies Do about Identity?

Kenneth Hoover

Global democratization seems to have foundered on the rock of "identity politics." In an era widely expected to have seen the triumph of democratic processes around the world, the substantive character of democracy seems now to be threatened. The nationalist response to terrorism evident in U.S. politics currently, the rising support for rightist parties in European elections, and the revolt powered by Islamic fundamentalism reveal profound stresses in democracies on questions of identity differences.

Tolerance, accommodation of difference, and progressive social policies seem to be giving way to limitations on rights, withdrawal of benefits and entitlements, and exclusionary, even chauvinist, posturing. Most often, the driving rationale is public concern about "others," whether immigrants, culturally distinct peoples, suspect dissidents, or marginalized groups of citizens. Target groups are demeaned and vilified as a way of consolidating the power of dominant elements of society. Democracy has spread widely, but is it shallow? Terrorist threats escalate tensions and reduce inhibitions about authoritarian solutions.

What would the "deepening of democracy" mean? There appear to be two dimensions, one procedural, the other substantive, according to an influential formulation by Larry Diamond.[1] The *procedural* dimension has to do with respect for "political rights, civil liberties, and constitutional constraints." The *substantive* dimension of democracy becomes apparent by its absence: "the more shallow, exclusive, unaccountable, and abusive of individual and group rights is the electoral regime, the more difficult it will be for that regime to become deeply legitimated at the mass level."[2] Diamond here refers to "political culture" as distinct from the formal processes of electoral politics. Implicitly, I would suggest, the substantive dimension centers on the relationship between democracy and identity.

97

Contemporary politics is increasingly driven by these two concepts: democracy and identity. There is an escalating insistence that major decisions be responsive to public views, whether through elections, referenda, or other processes of democratic deliberation and judgment. At the same time, identity has become the focal point of policy disputes over the treatment of differences between people arising from religion, gender, race, ethnicity, and class. Democratic processes are often the key to advancing claims of identity—they provide openings for aggrieved groups to mobilize and seek public recognition of their claims. The struggle for women's suffrage, then women's liberation, then equal opportunity and affirmative action, illustrates how crucial democracy can be to claims based in conceptions of identity.

Yet identities can be harshly dealt with by democracies. On the principle of majority rule, the repression of minorities, or the denial of distinctive claims for particular groups, can be the result of democratic policy-making procedures. Indeed, this is a theme that appears in what Diamond alludes to discussing the possibility of a "reverse wave" of democratization.[3] In the United States, affirmative action programs have come up against state referenda that seek to undermine affirmative action and the equitable treatment of immigrants. With the terrorist threat intensified, public support for civil liberties has dropped precipitously.

How can democracy and identity be reconciled? How can the dynamics of identity development be made to fit with democracy so as to generate the policies that would improve the human condition? Democracy depends on an *equality* of rights, yet identity appears to be about the *particularity* of claims by groups or individuals. The answer to this seeming dilemma contains the seeds of a larger understanding of an emerging politics of human development. First, however, we need to understand what identity is made of. What is it that people want from an identity? What does behavioral research tell us about the characteristics of identity formation? With these questions answered, we can turn to the challenge of fitting identity needs into a framework of democratic decision-making.

Identity and Democratic Theory

Hannah Pitkin in *Fortune Is a Woman* sets the task for political theorists:

> Thus the political theorist is concerned not merely with the philosophical problem of whether humans can ever break the causal chain of history to make a new beginning, but even more

with the political problem of how and where and with whom we might take action, given our present circumstances.[4]

Following on Pitkin' s suggestion, my task in this chapter is to sketch a conceptual approach, termed *identity relations analysis*, that tells us something about the difference between what we can change in our condition and what we cannot; and that establishes a basis for democratic action to resolve political problems toward the betterment of society.

The verb "sketch" is carefully chosen. This chapter will limn a perspective on identity that has a wide variety of applications to current discussions in democratic political theory. Within the frame of this sketch, there is room for little more than some suggestive lines of inquiry, and the occasional illustrative detail. It is intended more to evoke questions than to specify answers.

Democratic Pathways to Identity Formation

In the introduction to this volume, we set out a framework for bringing into focus the convergent streams of research on identity formation. The common dimensions of identity take the form of relations of *competence, community,* and *commitment.* When these relations are sturdy and authentic, when the impetus of the self in each respect meets the approbation of society on an honest basis, identity resides on a secure foundation. Yet identity is Janus-faced. It can bring us happiness and security, and it can bring us misery and a desire to dominate others. As a simple device for opening the analysis of what leads to which result, we likened identity to a three-legged stool resting on relations of competence, commitment, and community.

Which brings us to the troublesome question—is any three-legged stool as good as any other? The psychologists have an answer for this—or rather an observation confirmed by many findings. To appreciate the significance of this work, there is a need to understand something of the pattern of identity formation centered, as it is, in early adulthood—though with lifelong entailments, consequences, and elaborations. It turns out that there are differing degrees of stability in the stools upon which identity perches.

As we have seen in examining the empirical research, four patterns emerge: *Foreclosure*—the premature shutting down of the formation process; *Diffusion*—the failure to achieve a clear sense of identity; *Moratorium*—a phase of experimentation and testing; and *Achievement*—the situating of identity in firmly internalized relations. Individuals may go through varied combinations of these stages, though the research indicated that Moratorium, followed by Achievement, offers the prospect of the most durable form of identity. Diffusion is a painful and unstable condition, while Foreclosure delivers a result, but one that is subject to being undermined by a change of circumstance or setting.

So much for the social psychology of identity formation. The political implications are of interest here. Let me cite the relevant finding in James Marcia's summation of the research:

> One of the most consistent findings in identity status research has been that male and female Foreclosures, especially relative to Moratoriums, score highly on measures of authoritarianism and socially stereotypical thinking. They show preference for a strong leader over a democratic process, obedience over social protest, and the "pseudo-speciation" described by Erikson: firm conviction that "their" group and "their" way are right.[5]

A separate study based on the notorious Milgram experiments found the Foreclosures to be the most willing administrators of maximum electrical shocks to pseudosubjects in an obedience experiment.[6] This research illustrates that a world in which variously formed identities coexist is more likely to be free and peaceful if people live in societies where it is possible to form a durable sense of identity.

These findings bear importantly on a subtlety of the community dimension of identity—and of its significance for democracy. There exists a necessary tension between the *individual* and *universal* aspects of the communities involved in identity. Those who dwell entirely in a particular community with no conception of a larger universe of others who, though distinct in particulars, share a wider bond, risk the dangers of isolation and discrimination and/or fall prey to the temptations of chauvinism and aggression. Similarly, the attempt to situate an identity wholly in an undifferentiated universe seems to undermine the sense of personal coherence that identity promises, and which the psyche apparently requires. At the extremes, the particularist community is prone to foreclosure. Similarly, the unmediated universalist perspective can result in diffusion.

The empirical findings associating tolerance with identity achievement indicate that it is vital to be situated in *both* the particular *and* the universal aspects of community identification. A striking illustration of this point is Kristen Renwick Monroe's finding in *The Heart of Altruism* that the most altruistic people in her study, the rescuers of Jews from the Nazis, gave up nothing of the distinctive qualities of their own identities—they varied widely in background and none of them were Jews—while acting out of a complete commitment to a universalist perspective on human rights.[7] Both are needed to complete the repertoire of an identity. The suggestion is that each is essential somehow to the other.

A cautionary note: A plurality of identities is not necessarily the same as "identity confusion." "Nested" identities, to use political theorist David Miller' s phrase, are very likely the norm and may, indeed, be expressive of a robust personality. Successive layers of identification with, say, neighborhood, church, nation, and humanity are not only possible, but typical.

If, in short, one values democratic relations and voluntarism, there are indeed better and worse ways of acquiring an identity. The *leitmotiv* here is that individuals do indeed have to find their own identities, but that the processes of society are critical to the search—and these, if they are not designed properly, can lead to dysfunction and debilitation. The question becomes how to approach the social term of identity relations so as to bring about processes of Moratorium and Achievement rather than Foreclosure and Diffusion. The further question concerns the preservation of the initiative of the self in seeking a resilient and tolerable identity. The answers to these questions are of possible interest to theorists of democracy.

Implications of Identity Relations for Democracy

As you may guess, the main political implication of these findings is that there needs to be someplace for all of these contending identities to work through their differences and to find those arrangements of power, authority, and individual rights that make identity formation itself possible. The small difficulty here is that the nation-state, while it can provide the forum for many expressions that are necessary to this task, has to steer clear of the temptation to confer, and thereby foreclose, identities for groups or individuals.

It seems, at this point, that we have arrived at the dilemma stated by David Miller:

> In essence, identity politics is self-defeating, for it looks to politics to provide a formation of identities that the political sphere by its very nature cannot provide; and in encouraging groups to affirm their singular identities at the expense of shared national identities, it undermines the very conditions in which minority groups, especially disadvantaged groups, can hope to achieve some measure of justice for their demands.[8]

Let me give you my own reflections on this serious dilemma having, as I do, a critical attitude toward conventional conceptions of "identity politics." I think it is important to observe that each term of an identity relation carries with it the potential for negative and positive results (see figures 7.1 and 7.2). There are both highways and byways on the path to identity. Perhaps it is easiest to see the combination of possibilities in chart form:

	Individual Aspects	Social/Political Aspects
Competence	Ability, Motivation	Legitimation, Certification
Community	Gender, Ethnicity, Race, Region, Class, Religion, Ideology, etc.	Affirmation, Tolerance, Protected Expression
Commitment	Fidelity, Duty	Support for Sustaining Commitments

FIGURE 7.1 POSITIVE IDENTITY RELATIONS

	Individual Aspects	Social / Political Aspects
Competence	Fraud	False Recognition
Community	Chauvinism	Sexism, Racism, Pseudospeciation
Commitment	Domination, Violence	Disruption, Interference

FIGURE 7.2 NEGATIVE IDENTITY RELATIONS

The problem of democratic responses to the phenomena of identity is essentially a question of confronting the social/political aspects of both the positive and negative relations that characterize the struggle for identity. What these distinctions suggest is that the objective of those who would act together to improve the human condition might focus on four kinds of activities: the *provision* of constructive life choices; the *legitimation* of genuine competencies, communities, and commitments; the *prevention* of harmful behavior toward others arising from individual maladies of identity formation; and the *protection* of individual rights against abuses by states, corporations, groups and persons. I have charted these activities in figure 7.3.

Choice, the privileged category of human action in liberally influenced societies, appears here not as *morally privileged*, for some choices are morally execrable, but as *developmentally privileged*. The exercise of choice can, as is readily evident, be devastating to the self and to others. Empirical research tells us that the act of choosing facilitates growth and development if there are positive choices at hand. The foreclosure of choice, while it can prevent harm or abuse, rarely works to produce genuine competencies, authentic communities, or willing commitments. The issue for political theorists lies in protecting choice, to be sure, and *in assuring that there are good developmental alternatives available for choosing.*[9]

The most that a democratically governed society can do is to assure that good developmental alternatives are in place. What it *cannot* do at the risk of false competencies, artificial communities, and deniable commitments, is to force the choosing. Choices, once made, that involve dependency, as in familial relations, can usefully be sustained by well-deliberated policies of mediation and support. In this realm, a focus on recovery from bad choices is at least as important as promptings to follow the optimal path. Income security is a fundamental social insurance policy against the consequences of bad choices—a policy that keeps open the possibility of better choices in the future. Income security is also a protection against the vicissitudes of life that undermine even the best choices.

Another arena for common action involves using the coercive power of the state to reduce the harm arising from individual maladies of identity formation, such as fraud, chauvinism, domination, and violence. There are limits to interpersonal as well as cultural relativism, and those limits are revealed by an analysis of identity relations. Whether these abuses arise from bad choosing, or from bad alternatives, they have sad results for the self and others. While the state cannot often save us from ourselves for developmental reasons, it can, as John Stuart Mill so earnestly proclaimed, try to save us from each other. To prevent harm, certain choices have to be outlawed. Similarly, governance must focus on the

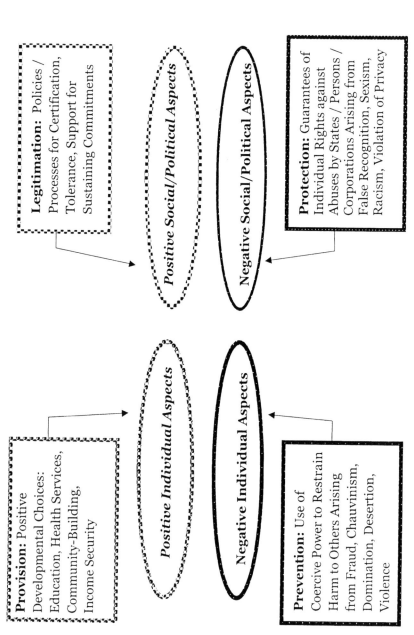

Legitimation: Policies / Processes for Certification, Tolerance, Support for Sustaining Commitments

Positive Social/Political Aspects

Negative Social/Political Aspects

Protection: Guarantees of Individual Rights against Abuses by States / Persons / Corporations Arising from False Recognition, Sexism, Racism, Violation of Privacy

Provision: Positive Developmental Choices: Education, Health Services, Community-Building, Income Security

Positive Individual Aspects

Negative Individual Aspects

Prevention: Use of Coercive Power to Restrain Harm to Others Arising from Fraud, Chauvinism, Domination, Desertion, Violence

FIGURE 7.3 GOVERNANCE AND IDENTITY RELATIONS

protection of individual rights through fundamental legislation so that individuals are not victimized by false recognition, sexism, racism, and the violation of privacy.

By the same analysis, it is apparent that the least auspicious arena for collective action involves the reformation of individual identity-seeking strategies. If we have learned anything from the political experience of the last few centuries, it is that reformations bring inquisitions, and state-sponsored therapy carries heavy dangers. Here is where Pitkin' s line between what can be changed, and what cannot, might well be drawn. It is not so much that individuals cannot be shaped in positive ways, it is that coercive collective action is the wrong means to the end. Reformation, even redemption, privately sought is one thing; a visit from an agent of the state is another. An identity built, or changed, on the basis of the former has a better chance of durability than one foreclosed, or enforced, by the state. The *process* of identity formation has important consequences for the *content* of identity—in particular for its political content.

The best role for the state on the constructive and affirmative side of governance is to improve the choices available to individuals, and to guarantee the freedom to make those choices. Part of that task includes the provision of authentic processes of certification and legitimation. Tolerance and the protection of expression are worthy goals of legislation. Affirmative legislation is also needed to make the keeping of commitments easier, or at least to limit the disruption of those commitments.[10] These are substantive measures that contribute to the formation of democratic identities.

While political theorists of the modern era seem less interested in thinking constructively about the coercive side of governance, it is vital that there be a considered perspective here as well. Societies where coercion is left to the tides of opinion wind up with capital punishment even in the presence of evidence that it is unfairly administered. Vindictiveness replaces justice and degrades claims of due process. Conventional theories focus on the prevention of harm without illuminating much of what harm consists of. Developmental findings offer some substantive suggestions for legislators and citizen activists, as we have illustrated in the chart above. Similarly, those who would protect rights can learn a bit about what rights have to be protected from. *Physical* harm and abuse is relatively easy to understand; *developmental* harm and abuse requires rather more investigation.

So much for governmental policies. There are other institutions to consider. This framework for analyzing identity relations has implications for the market as well. As I have argued elsewhere:

> The market rewards capital, whether acquired by labor, fraud, chance, inheritance, or the proceeds of a monopolistic or oligopolistic position in the marketplace. All but the first of these has no standing in developmental theory, with the exception of those limited forms of inheritance that contribute to the maintenance of the family. The forces of capital reinforced by political power can violate developmental norms just as surely as egalitarian regimes intent on erasing authentic differences among people.
>
> The problem is not with the market as a device, but rather with the substitution of market devices for other social and political processes that are essential to human development. The practices and customs of civil society that give relations of commitment a higher priority than individual material advancement, for example, are characteristic of a *civil*-ized society. That is why the family enjoys a protected status that constrains individual choices about the use of one' s material resources.[11]

The point is that identity relations analysis offers a putative theory of market regulation and constraint. Viewed from a developmental perspective, those aspects of the market that encourage the cultivation and maintenance of competence, community, and commitment are socially beneficial. Those forms of buying and selling that undermine identity formation and maintenance are harmful. We know that limits must be placed on child labor, for example, because it can undermine education and health—both critical to achieving competence in a broad array of human activities.

However, the market has its developmental uses as well. An environment of experimentation and risk-taking generates challenges. The mobilization of individual knowledge and the harnessing of private energies leads into productive relations between the self and society. Adam Smith was right about the market as an arena for seeking respect, both for ourselves, and from others.

> To deserve, to acquire, and to enjoy the respect and admiration of mankind, are the great objects of ambition and emulation. Two different roads are presented to us, equally leading to the attainment of this so much desired object; the one, by the study of wisdom and the practice of virtue; the other, by the acquisition of wealth and greatness.[12]

Adam Smith did not approve, nor would a developmental theorist, of every stratagem for gaining respect—or a sense of identity. The best stratagems from Smith' s point of view are those of "a select, though, I am afraid, but a small party, who are the real and steady admirers of wisdom and virtue."¹³ Not all stratagems contribute to the true wealth of a nation, Smith seems to be saying, only those that do verily enrich one' s character and the quality of relations in society. Nevertheless, he saw the market as a means of providing for the wise and the foolish alike.

In the pursuit of qualitative improvement in a democracy, then, the market alone, by Smith' s admission, will not be sufficient. *A constitutionally bounded deliberative democracy seems to offer the best prospect for engaging individuals in the mediation and refinement of developmental choices, while limiting the role of coercion to the protection of life and of the integrity of the self.*¹⁴

Those who point to the potential abuses of the coercive power of government, such as Friedrich Hayek, often overlook the abusive practices found in an unconstrained market. As George Orwell said of Hayek' s *Road to Serfdom*, "[Hayek] does not see, or will not admit, that a return to ' free' competition means for the great mass of people a tyranny probably worse, because more irresponsible, than that of the state."¹⁵ The private autocracies of the economy can be just as coercive as the cultural practices of a society. The democratic state exists to provide a constituted arena where people with differing economic and cultural interests can meet, find common ground, and seek the mutual improvement of the human condition. The safeguards against arbitrary uses of power are made evident so that accountability can be exercised.

The markers of identity formation discussed here admit of many variations and combinations, and this provides one more justification for distinctive communities and nations. To use David Miller' s distinction, the *social* justice of each community, if it truly nurtures a humane process of identity development, will contribute to the emergence of *global* justice by producing citizens who are of a mind to balance the needs of a particular identity with the universal requirements of global comity. In examining the prospects for social justice, Miller foresees that "What is required for the pursuit of social justice is not the elimination of cultural differences, but the opening up of national identities so that they become accessible to the members of many (ideally all) cultural groups within existing democratic states."¹⁶ Those who see identity as having to be singular and coherent if it is to be robust, may have trouble with this formulation. However, the research cited here suggests that the most tolerant identity, perhaps the identity most disposed to social justice in all its forms, is one that is secure in *both* individual identifications and in one or more universalizing frameworks as well.

In the end, it is not sufficient merely to specify, in Pitkin' s phrase, "how and where and with whom we might take action, given our present circumstances." It is essential that we understand what sort of action would most likely bring us to together rather than drive us apart. Identity is not optional. People will seek an identity whether by fair means or foul, constructive or destructive. The vital mission of a democratic society is the provision of institutions, practices, and developmental choices that meet the shared need for identity, while fostering the best in human development.

In conclusion, we return to the birth of democracy. As Cynthia Farrar reminds us, in Athenian society, "Justice is legitimated if it is shown to be essential to personal well-being. Athenian political life raised the possibility of maintaining a bracing tension between personal and civic identity."[17] The *substantive* democratization of nondemocratic societies requires that this tension be worked through in all spheres of society: the state, the market, and the civil society. The first step is to understand the nature of the tension. Erik Erikson set us upon the road to that understanding.

Notes

1. "Is The Third Wave Over?" *Journal of Democracy* 7 (1996): 20–37. Cf. S. Huntington, "After Twenty Years: The Future of the Third Wave," *Journal of Democracy* 8 (1997): 3–12. For a fuller specification of Diamond's model of liberal democracy, see *Developing Democracy: Toward Consolidation*. Baltimore, MD: Johns Hopkins University Press, 1999, 10–13.

2. *Ident.*, 34. In *Developing Democracy*, Diamond assesses the comparative data on the cultural legitimation of democracy, specif. ch. 5.

3. *Ident.*, 35.

4. H. Pitkin. *Fortune Is a Woman: Gender and Politics in the Thought of Niccoló Machiavelli, with a New Afterword*. Chicago: University of Chicago Press, 1999, 290.

5. J. Marcia in Hoover et al. *op. cit.*, 87.

6. *Ident.*

7. *The Heart of Altruism: Perceptions of a Common Humanity*. Princeton, NJ: Princeton University Press, 1996.

8. D. Miller. *Citizenship and National Identity*, Cambridge, England: Polity Press, 2000, 79.

9. Raymond Plant points out that Friedrich Hayek's commitment to individual freedom does not extend to authorizing government to assure that good choices are available to all. See R. Plant, "Hirsch, Hayek and Habermas: Dilemmas of Distribution," in *Dilemmas of Liberal Democracies: Studies in Fred Hirsch's Social Limits to Growth*, eds. A. Ellis and K. Kumar. London: Tavistock, 1983, 45–64. By contrast, Amartya Sen makes the provision of choices the thesis of his *Development as Freedom*, Oxford: Oxford University Press, 1999.

10. Cf. Giddens' point about *emancipatory* politics and *life* politics, the former involving the release from burdens of oppression, and the latter the possibility of choosing a way of life that meets inner needs for expression and fulfillment. Feminist theory is seen to illustrate the possibilities of life politics. *Op. cit.*, 214–15. Giddens' work centers on what are noted here as *positive* aspects of identity development. I find it necessary to add an analysis of the political implications of *negative* aspects as well.

11. Hoover et al. *op. cit.*, 50. Cf. This is a point that Hegel understood early in the evolution of thought about modern political economy. See J. Muller, *The Mind and the Market: Capitalism in Modern European Thought*, New York: Knopf, 2002, chapter 6.

12. A. Smith. *The Theory of Moral Sentiments*, in R. L. Meek, D. D. Raphael, P. G. Stein, eds., *The Glasgow Edition of the Works and Correspondence of Adam Smith*. Indianapolis, IN: Liberty Fund, 1984, 86.

13. *Ident.*

14. Cf. Miller, *op. cit.*, 161–79; K. Hoover with V. Johnson, J. Miles, and S. Weir. *Ideology and Political Life*, 3rd ed. Belmont, CA: Wadsworth/Thompson, 2001, Part Two, 149–212.

15. In N. Annan, *Our Age: The Generation That Made Post-War Britain*, London: Fontana, 1990, 586. Cf. K. Hoover, *Economics as Ideology: Keynes, Laski, Hayek, and the Creation of Contemporary Politics*, Rowman & Littlefield, 2003.

16. D. Miller. *Principles of Social Justice*. Cambridge, MA: Harvard University Press, 1999, 263.

17. C. Farrar. "Ancient Greek Political Theory as a Response to Democracy," in John Dunn, ed., *Democracy: The Unfinished Journey 508 BC to AD 1993*. Oxford, England: Oxford University Press, 1992, 17–39.

Chapter Eight

Globalization, Identity, and the Search for Chosen Traumas

Catarina Kinnvall

This chapter proceeds from, and develops, aspects of Erik Erikson's notion of identity crisis in which ego-identity comes into conflict with psycho-social relations. Building on Giddens' and Bauman's work on globalization and the politics of belonging, I show how these psycho-social relations have changed as a result of globalization. Globalization, as spelled out in the chapter, has affected individuals' personal security and rootedness in the world and has left the individual at a loss in a world in which she or he lacks the psychological support provided by traditional societal structures.

The chapter begins by considering this relationship between globalization and increased ontological insecurity. It then proceeds with the following two aims. First it seeks to analyze the extent to which, and how, such increased ontological insecurity and existential anxiety have intensified the search for stable identities so as to avoid disruptive selves. This involves a reinvestigation of Erikson's discussion of anxiety disorders and how self-identity is brought into harmony with social definitions of identity. Second, it attempts to explain, in the light of globalization, the consequences of this search for a stable identity for group conflict. In doing this I show how the use of real or imagined traumas becomes an essential part of the group's construction of self and how such traumas are increasingly used in the dehumanization process of the other. The focus on traumas helps us in explaining the psychological (and real) implications of insecurity and group conflict.

In doing this the chapter departs from both essentialist and instrumentalist approaches to identity at the same time as it problematizes the constructivist approach by giving attention to socio-psychological aspects of category formation and the essentialization of the "other." Here the studies of Julia Kristeva and Vamik Volkan on the psychological foundations of the dehumanization of the "other" have proven useful for reinterpreting Erikson's work on identity crisis and insecurity. The chapter thus shows how Erikson's work provides a firm foundation from which to build, understand, and analyze the processes behind groups' constructions of homogenous selves and enemy others in a global era.

Globalization, Ontological Security, and the Search for Stable Identities

The effects of globalization have been debated in much recent literature,[1] and it is quite clear from these debates that globalization is not a new event. However, the various processes of globalization have involved a number of recent changes in terms of *speed, scale,* and *cognition* (Kinnvall, 2002a; Manners, 2000). The compression of time and space has taken on novel dimensions and the number of economic, political, social, and human linkages between societies is greater than at any previous point in history. The globe is also increasingly being viewed as a smaller place with events elsewhere having consequences for our everyday political, social, and economic lives. Together these changes in speed, scale, and cognition affect individuals' sense of being. Everyday life changes through this deterritorialization of time and space as in a world of diminishing territorial barriers, the search for constant time- and space-bound identities have become a way to cope with the impacts of modern life (Harvey, 1993, 4).

Globalization has, in other words, some real social, political, and economic consequences. The effects of a number of transformative processes, such as capitalist development, media overflow, structural adjustment policies, privatization, urbanization, unemployment, and forced migration have for many people created a rootlessness and a loss of stability. Here it is important to note how the process of globalization is often accompanied by a "neoliberal" ideology all over the world (see Bauman, 2001; Calhoun, 1994; Scholte, 2000). Indeed, as Scholte has noted, the considerable negative impacts of globalization have resulted mainly from neoliberal policies toward the trend. This is similar to Giddens' (1990) argument that modernization is a fundamental part of globalization. Globalization in this wider sense has had important repercussions for various dimensions of human security in terms of economic, ecological, and military security–all of which have cultural and psychological consequences.

First of all, this emerging ideology has often changed the role of the state from a welfare provider to a market competitor. The result has frequently been an authority vacuum in which new leaders have come forth in response to individuals' desire for security and welfare. Such groups and leaders tend to provide a challenge to the state as witnessed by everything from nationalist claims to ethnic and religious calls for autonomy and recognition, to antiglobalization campaigns. To this can be added recent attempts to democratize societies where the norms of equality and egalitarianism have tended to delegitimize previous hierarchical power relations in society. Some basic consequences of this are that (1) old ways of getting things done are being eliminated, which tends to leave behind only uncertainty, and (2) the structures that identified the community and bound it together are also being eliminated, which has a disintegrative effect.[2]

The democratic electoral process also helps to mobilize groups that have previously been rather passive and weak, and often leaders tend to polarize issues to attract political followers. Simultaneously, constitutional guarantees of freedom of association and expression also provide political space to extremist organizations that may be openly antidemocratic, divisive, and violent (Kolodner, 1995). It is not uncommon that such groups mobilize against immigrants or other (often) marginalized groups in society. This becomes particularly evident in times of rapid change and economic recession.

Second, trade liberalization in the form of structural adjustment policies (SAPs) has repeatedly deprived the state of its main source of income (taxes), which in turn has made it more difficult for the public sector to effectively alleviate poverty (Scholte, 2000). These programs, aimed at privatization and increased global competitiveness, were meant to create stability and to strengthen civil society but have often had the reverse effect by removing job security for many, thus aggravating social tension (Calhoun, 1994; Hoogvelt, 2001; Hurrell and Woods, 1999; Kolodner, 1995; Scholte, 2000). According to UN estimates, around 800 million people of the world's work force of 2.8 billion people, were unemployed in the early 1990s while 700 millions were underemployed (Simai, 1995, 4). Job losses in the rich societies have regularly followed upon the introduction of labor-saving technologies together with the tendency among many firms to use global advantages as an excuse for moving manufacturing plants to low-wage societies.

The ability of many transnational companies to move at a short notice without taking the consequences of such moves has, according to Bauman (1998), created a new class of "absentee landlords." This ability has accelerated insecurity for many, particularly in the South. Furthermore, the debt crisis in regards to global loans to the South has undermined the capacity for many of these countries in their struggles against poverty. To this can be added how the volatility of global financial markets has increased insecurity among both the rich and the poor societies.

Third, the emergence of global social ecology has had a number of damaging consequences. Hence despite the fact that we now have sophisticated tools for anticipating and monitoring natural disasters and ecological trends, the technologies of globalization have also increased pollution and paper use and have created new outlets for waste, tobacco products, pharmaceutical, and pesticides. Popular panics in regards to the spread of HIV/AIDS, BSE, and genetically modified foods, have been accompanied with widespread fears of rapid growth in world population (Scholte, 2000). Ecological insecurity has thus increasingly come to permeate the contemporary human condition.

Fourth, globalization and militarization have been closely linked in many ways. Computer networks have become a key tool of contemporary warfare and global reach with "rapid reaction forces" has facilitated military interventions by the North in conflicts in the South and the East. Global finance has also been heavily involved in paying for major wars, such as the Gulf War of 1990–91, and global companies have remained main producers of military equipment with traders supplying arms to both weak states and to rebels (Scholte, 2000). Rather than equating globalization with peace (which is not to diminish the number of peace organization that have arisen in its wake), the linkage between globalization and militarization has hence, in many ways, heightened human insecurity.

Finally, globalization has become intimately linked with migration and urbanization. Together these have created new class divisions as well as changed divisions of labor. Migration, in this sense, is both a structural and a psychological process. It is often characterized by a sense of powerlessness and dependence as insecurity is increasing among many migrants. This is frequently mixed with an acute anxiety about their new circumstances and strong feelings of homelessness (see Bauman, 2001; Castles and Davidson, 2000; Ong, 1999). The fact that many of these people find themselves both structurally marginalized and ontologically insecure often gives rise to a politics of resistance and the growth of local identities.

The result of all this is an increasing feeling of dislocation for many people. These global changes have deprived many of the protective cocoon of relational ties that safeguarded community members and groups in the past (Giddens, 1990). In this wider sense, globalization tends to break down

> the protective framework of the small community and of tradition replacing these with many larger, impersonal organizations. The individual feels bereft and alone in a world in which she or he lacks the psychological supports and the sense of security provided by more traditional settings. (Giddens, 1991, 33)

Modern society has made the lives of more individuals migratory and mobile as they are uprooted from their original social environment or from traditional ways of living. The result has been increasing attempts to "de-modernize" in order to seek "reversal of the modern trend that have left the individual 'alienated' and beset with the threats of meaninglessness" (Berger in Pathak, 1998, 22). This leads to what Berger calls "homelessness." This homelessness, Berger argues, has found its most devastating expression in the area of religion.

> The de-modernizing impulse, whether it looks backwards into the past or forwards into the future, seeks a reversal of the modern trends that have left the individual "alienated" and beset with the threats of meaninglessness. (Berger in Pathak, 1998, 22)

Here, Giddens argues that in the past, the particularities of time and space merged with religion and mythology to create a "privileging of place." An identity based upon one's place within such a locality provided personal security and "rootedness" in the world, or at least security against the anxiety of identity crisis (Giddens, 1991, 26). Going back to such an imagined past is thus an attempt to recreate a lost sense of security.

Ontological security refers to a "person's fundamental sense of safety in the world and includes a basic trust of other people. Obtaining such trust becomes necessary in order for a person to maintain a sense of psychological well-being and avoid existential anxiety" (Giddens, 1991, 38–39). Ontological security is, in other words, a security of being, a sense of confidence and trust that the world is what it appears to be. Trust of other people is like an emotional inoculation against existential anxieties—"a protection against future threat and dangers which allows the individual to sustain hope and courage in the face of whatever debilitating circumstances she or he might later confront" (Giddens, 1991, 39). In this Giddens relies on Erikson (1950), whose approach to identity signifies the closeness between identity and security. Identity, in Erikson's work, is seen as an anxiety-controlling mechanism reinforcing a sense of trust, predictability, and control in reaction to disruptive change by reestablishing a previous identity or formulating a new one.

For Giddens then, like Erikson, self-identity consists of the development of a consistent feeling of biographical continuity where the individual is able to sustain a narrative about the self and answer questions about doing, acting, and being. Maintaining such a narrative is not easy, however, as the literature on globalization, diaspora, refugees, and migration has shown. Giddens' notions of ontological security and existential anxiety are thus fruitful for understanding the global-local nexus as psychologized discourses of domination and resistance. Globalization has made it more difficult, but not less desirable, to think in terms of singular, integrated and harmonious identities as individuals constantly tune their actions to an increasing number of others and issues.

A Contemporary Reading of Erik Erikson: Anxiety Disorders and Social Selves

For a better understanding of this increased desire for one stable identity, Erikson's move away from a Freudian preoccupation with the unconscious to the conscious, is useful. In this he describes a developmental model in which identity must be harmonized to fit in with the social context. Identity, in Erikson's terminology, is expressed both internally (private) and externally (public). As two mutually constituted processes they unavoidably come into conflict with each other as an individual ages and as her social circumstances change. The actual process is explained as one in which the child and then the adult go through different stages of development, where every stage results in an identity crisis in which the self-identity comes into conflict with the individual's psycho-social relations. To avoid personality disorders, the individual constantly has to adapt the picture she has of herself to fit in with new societal definitions of her own identity. As the environment is changing its demands, the individual goes through an identity crisis as she can no longer make reality correspond with the picture she has of herself. She experiences a strong feeling of dissonance. As she feels incapable of countering this new reality, her ontological security is threatened. The result of such identity crises is identity development (Erikson, 1950).

Erikson is viewed as being the first person who used identity as a term in psychological analysis. Despite the novelty of his approach, however, few authors within the broad literature on identity have made use of his work. This may have to do with the suggestion that he describes the social context in a rather reductionist way, meaning that the context is reduced to the individual level rather than to the structural level. In this sense his concern is that of belongingnessless rather than that of modes of belonging. As Tony Smith (1976) has noted, for Erikson a stable personality structure depends on a stable social structure in which roles regulate human interaction and through which individuals become predictable to each other and to themselves.

This conception of the relationship between humans and society differs from more structural analyses. Laing, for instance, believes that the induction into established social roles is a process of alienation where the individual gets alienated from herself and from others through the emergence of a superstructure—society (in Smith, 1976). And those schooled in a Marxist tradition would insist that the preoccupation with belonginglessness is ideological in the sense that it sees the origin of human misery in the breakdown of an established system, rather than in its per-petuation. Indeed, as Smith (1976) notes, there is in Erikson's work a cer-tain nostalgia for tradition and order in society, even when such an order takes an explicit feudal form. As Erikson's description of the Indian soci-ety reveals:

> There was a time in India when servants, passing from father to son, used to serve in the same family for generations. They were regarded and treated as members of the family. They suf-fered with the employers in their misfortunes and the latter shared the servants' joys and sorrows. In those days, India was reputed for a social order free from friction and this order en-dured for thousands of years on that basis. (Erikson, 1969, 340)

This "conservative bias" means, according to Kovel (1974), that truly radical change is put aside, that all that is "undone" is the most obvious excesses of the existing order while the order itself remains unchanged.

I agree with this criticism. However, in contrast to Smith and Kovel, I do not see such a clear dividing line between either the order-disorder aspect or the individual and the structural in Erikson's work. First of all, there are all sorts of ways to carry out radical change. As Lipsitz and Kritzer (1975, 721) have noted, it is possible to practice land reform with-out liquidating the owners, or changing political structures without im-prisoning the opposition, or for that matter being a socialist without be-ing a Stalinist. Second, the above quote may imply a romanticization of a stable structure, but it also points to the dislocating effects of the break-down of such societal structures. Understanding the psychological con-sequences of this kind of structural disordering is in many ways funda-mental for appreciating how ontological insecurity and existential anxiety can result in the search for one stable identity. There exists, as Roberta Sigel (1989, 459) has noted, "in humans a powerful drive to maintain the sense of one's identity, a sense of continuity that allays fear of changing too fast or being changed against one's will by outside forces." To attain a workable psycho-social equilibrium, Erikson therefore maintains that one needs to find recourse in an identity that is safely anchored in a cul-tural context. Without such anchorage, the personal identity will be un-able to function and thrive and will instead show signs of "disorder, dys-function, disintegration, anomie" (Erikson, 1964, 139).

Hence, Erikson defines personal identity as a process "located" in the core of the individual at the same time as it can be found in the core of the communal culture, a "process which establishes, in fact, the iden-tity of these two identities" (Erikson, 1968, 22). This means that any con-cept of personal identity must, by definition, be socially integrated as a stable identity demands "a confidence that the inner sameness and continuity prepared in the past (for oneself) is matched by the sameness and continuity of one's meaning for others" (Erikson, 1950, 261). Ego-identity for Erikson, is therefore a lot more than the search for a core self, it is both "a subjective experience, and as a dynamic fact, a group psychological phenomenon" (Erikson, 1959, 22).

As Erikson himself phrased it in a personal conversation with Margareth Brenman-Gibson (1997:332) regarding the search for the idea of a Self with a capital "S." "Yes, I have thought about that a great deal and have even thought of discarding the term 'ego-identity' entirely . . . in fact I have the thought that the whole 'Self,' with a capital 'S,' probably includes several 'selves.'" In this Erikson comes closer to a number of post-structuralist and postmodernist thinkers than he, perhaps, may have wished.[3] Writers within these traditions (see, for example, Calhoun, 1995; Gergen, 1999; Hall, 1992) would insist that the individual search for one stable identity does not mean that such identities actually exist. Rather, as Stuart Hall has argued, we need to understand identity, not as a fixed, natural state of being, but as a *process of becoming.* "If we feel that we have a unified identity from birth to death, it is only because we construct a comforting story or 'narrative about the self,' about ourselves" (1992, 227). This implies that internalized self-notions can never be separated from self/other representations and that such notions are always responsive to new interpersonal relationships (Ogilvie and Ashmore, 1991, 230).

Erikson's refusal to separate out culture and society from a construction of self, is thus a very novel approach for someone writing in the early 1950s. In relating development to personal relationships throughout an individual's cultural and social life cycle, Erikson problematizes much psychoanalytic theory that tends to reduce societal influence to mother-infant relations. At the same time he also questions a common tendency to view autonomy as some kind of developmental end point. Many societies outside the Northern American context do not have self-realization, self-assertiveness, and personal confrontation as defining parameters for interpersonal communication and action. Furthermore, and perhaps more importantly for the purpose of this chapter, by going beyond the oedipal stage, Erikson actually provides a means for interpreting the structural insecurities arising in the borderlines between the global and the local: the global-local nexus.

Globalization as a technological annulment of temporal/spatial distances does not, in other words, so much homogenize the human condition as it tends to polarize it. As Bauman has noted, such polarization "augurs freedom of meaning-creation for some, but portends ascription to meaninglessness for others. Some can now move out of the locality—any locality—at will. Others watch helplessly the sole locality they inhabit moving away from under their feet" (Bauman, 1998, 18). This is what

Bauman (1998) refers to as "symmetrical differentiation," namely that while the elites increasingly choose isolation (physical or mental "gated communities"), the rest of the population finds itself excluded and forced to pay the cultural, psychological and political price for their new isolation.

This is where it is important to bring to light Erikson's (1959, 1982) concept of generativity, which is a fundamental part of his view on the life cycle. This concept refers to the capacity to provide for successive generations where failure to do so results in its opposite—stagnation. Stagnation, as Eagle has noted, creates resentment and hostility (against immigrants, against the poor, the weak or the "deviant") and is likely to ensue in the retreat to local identities; a 'retreat to the private and the personal' (Eagle, 1997, 344). As Erikson himself puts it, stagnation involves "the symptomatology of some of the psychological disorders which during a given period prevail in a substantial minority of the population." It represents "the *epidemiological counterparts* to the *dominant ethos* of a period's pattern of communality and productivity" (Erikson, 1959, 12, his emphasis; c.f. Eagle, 1997, 344). The actual life cycle is hence a system of generation and regeneration that is given continuity by domestic, professional and other institutions.

When this continuity breaks down, when we find ourselves in a "far-away" place or space, physically and/or mentally, we are in a process of stagnation. "'(F)ar-away' space is an unnerving experience; venturing 'far-away' means being beyond one's ken, out of place and out of one's element, inviting trouble and fearing harm" (Bauman, 1998, 13). Stagnation works, in other words, as a form of adaptation to the new circumstances created by globalization. This makes it more likely that the next stage of development life challenges will be met by despair rather than by integrity, making the eruption of hostility, destructiveness, and the dehumanization of the other increasingly likely.

Here I find Erikson's notion of pseudo-speciation especially helpful for understanding group conflict and social violence. The term pseudo-speciation, he argues (1964, 431):

> denotes the fact that while man is obviously one species, he appears on the scene split into groups (from tribes to nations, from castes to classes, from religions to ideologies) which provide their members with a firm sense of distinct and superior identity and immortality. This demands, however, that each group must invent for itself a place and moment in the very centre of the universe where and when an especially provident deity caused it to be created superior to all others, the mere mortals.

What Erikson is suggesting here is that the consequences of a disabling ego functioning is the emerging of totalism—of a well-defined place in this very center of the universe. "Where the human being despairs of an essential wholeness, he re-structures himself and the world by taking refuge in totalism" (Erikson, 1959, 133). By totalism he means "Gestalt in which an absolute boundary is emphasized . . . nothing that belongs inside must be left outside; nothing that must be outside should be tolerated inside" (1959, 133). Wherever this process of pseudo-speciation take place, when one's own group is regarded as superior while other groups are made into nonhumans, there is always the danger of total violence. This is when the killing of enemies becomes a glorious affirmation of group identity, rather than a regrettable necessity (Lipsitz and Kritzer, 1975). Thus, in the creation of clearly demarcated boundaries between self and other those who do not (seem to) subscribe to a common belief system thus challenge the very foundation of the group. "Like a besieged city, the movement must strengthen its walls against the enemy without and search for enemies within. True belief does not permit question and doubt" (Robins and Post, 1997, 94–95).

This emphasis on wholeness as seeming to "connote an assembly of parts," "that enter into fruitful association and organization" (Erikson, 1964, 92), has by some been taken to account for Erikson's attempts to establish a cohesive agent at the core of psychic functioning—an autonomous self (see for example McBride, 1990; Wurgaft, 1995). It has been argued that Erikson remains wedded to an idea of universal history that struggles against divisive "pseudo-identities" in the interest of more inclusive identities (Wurgaft 1995). The stage-structured approach in Erikson's work, has also been criticized for being rigid, deterministic, and normative in its hierarchy of stage-specific traits (e.g., Dannefer, 1984; Weiland, 1993). A number of scholars have, furthermore, pointed to the lack of women represented in Erikson's work and the tendency to portray identity as the development of autonomy, independence, and assertiveness, themes that run counter to the female experience (e.g., Gilligan, 1982; Marcia, 1980; Orlofsky, 1977).

Erikson was certainly a product of his time and the totalizing intentions of his life cycle approach does take on an air of universality and essentialism. He also looked most closely at the experience of men rather than that of women. However, at the same time he repeatedly emphasized the effects of history and the historical moment and was acutely aware of the differential shaping influences of different societies' value frames. This is true not only in regards to development, but also in regards to how theorists, researchers, and clinicians conceptualize it (see McFadden, 1999). The dialectical nature of Erikson's life cycle also tends to be a little more complex than the way it is commonly portrayed. Hence Elisabeth Horst (1995) notes that Erikson defines his stages in terms of conflicts or crises, rather than seeing each stage as being a single representation of identity. This means that the individual deals with the eight crises of the life cycle both sequentially and concurrently. She also argues against what she considers to be a misperception among many feminists and others in regards to Erikson's descriptions of identity and intimacy as one belonging to the male domain and one to the female.

Erikson never intended identity and intimacy to represent the polar opposites of separateness and connection. Returning to Erikson's discussion of intimacy, we find that balancing the tension between separateness and connection is the essence of the intimacy task. The polarity belongs within the intimacy task, not between the tasks of identity and intimacy. Separateness and autonomy as they are used by these authors do not correspond to the syntonic element of the identity task, but rather to the dystonic element of the intimacy task, isolation (Horst, 1995, 275–76).

Identity is in other words inseparable from intimacy and relationships and pseudospeciation is an integrated aspect of identity construction. "Today we know that all this has evolved together and must be studied together: social identity and the hatred or 'otherness', morality and righteous violence, inventiveness and mass murder" (Erikson, 1950, 430). Cultural, social, and economic instability makes it difficult to balance identity and identity confusion with the result that intimacy becomes more difficult than separateness:

> Identity formation involves a continuous conflict with powerful negative identity elements: what we know or fear or are told we are but try not to be or see; and what we consequently see in exaggeration in others. In times of aggravated crises all this can arouse in man a murderous hate of all kind of "otherness," in strangers and in himself. (Erikson, 1968, 289)

In sum, I believe that, despite recognizing a number of problematic aspects of Erikson's work, his emphasis on culture, context, historical significance, generativity, relationship, and intimacy together with his complex treatment of identity crises, pseudo-speciation, and totalism, do provide a fruitful and contemporary foundation from which to understand the relationship between globalization, ontological security and group conflict. The search for one stable identity (regardless of its actual existence) is a way to cope with an increasingly globalized world. In this process the need to construct an "other" who can be turned from stranger into enemy becomes a way to confirm the identity of oneself. The works of Vamik Volkan and Julia Kristeva are especially helpful for understanding these complex processes.

Chosen Traumas and Group Conflict:
The Dehumanization of "Others"

While there are many dissimilarities between the workings of the individual and the group mind, the tools of psychology, and especially of psychoanalysis, can shed light on group identity and behavior, not because they concern our unconscious drives or paths of psychosexual development, but because of the tacit assumption that each individual or group has complex and idiosyncratic ways of dealing with the demands of the inner and outer world (Volkan, 1997, 20).

In situations when individuals experience few opportunities for or sense of contribution, participation and growth at either a personal or a societal level, frustration is likely to lead to resentment and hostility (Eagle, 1997). It is in these circumstances that individuals become concerned with group identity. Individuals are usually not concerned with their large-group identity until it is threatened. "When a group is in continuing conflict or even at war with a neighbor group, members become acutely aware of their large-group identity to a point where it may far outweigh any concern for individual needs, even survival" (Volkan, 1997, 25). It is like breathing, Volkan argues, most of us are unaware of our breathing when our lungs function normally, but should we catch pneumonia we suddenly notice every breath. Similarly, the resisting subject may arise out of a sense of powerlessness or alienation as she becomes aware of unfair exclusion, whether political, economic, or social.

Volkan uses object-relations theory to account for how we externalize and project our unwanted elements onto enemies. Departing with Freud's notion of group psychology as consisting of individuals who seek to satisfy the same vital needs through idealization, identification and love of the group based primarily on the Oedipus complex, Volkan suggests the analogy of a large-scale tent to explore large-group psychology in a more comprehensive way. He invites us to think in terms of learning to wear, from childhood on, two layers of clothing where the first layer fits snugly (the personal identity), while the second layer is a loose covering that protects the individual in the way a parent, close family member, or other caregiver protects one (the ethnic, emotionally bonded large group). Because this garment is not formfitting, it also shelters other members of the group and thus resembles a large canvas tent. The members are not, as in Freud's interpretation, connected to each other because they love the same leader, but because they share the second layer while still wearing the first one. It is the leader's (the pole's) task to prevent the tent from collapsing, and in times of shared anxiety and regression the members rally around the pole and become preoccupied with repairing and mending the tears in the canvas of the large-group tent (Volkan, 1997, 27–29).

The individuals in the tent invest in shared reservoirs—for example, the flag, the song, the sauna—of psychological DNA in the canvas of the tent, but over time a shared way of feeling about one's large group becomes more important than the concrete symbols themselves. The introduction of traumatic events is likely to raise anxiety in the tent and may jeopardize the collective sense of self. The response can be of at least three kinds and can be directed inward toward one's own large canvas tent or outward toward another small or large tent. One possible response is repression, another is externalization, and a third is the broader concept of projection. Repression basically entails hiding away unwanted fragments of the self while externalization may be simple denial, suggesting that the self is not responsible for an emotion or action, but rather that an object "other" is to blame. Projection, finally, requires not only denial but includes the projection of unacceptable thought onto an other (Volkan, 1997, 89–101). "Because we externalize and project our unwanted elements onto enemies, they are also products of our fantasies" (Volkan, 1997, 107). This implies that there is a striking resemblance between self and other, precisely because the other has been invested with the unwanted traits of the self.

> Because the enemy is a reservoir of unwanted self and object representations within which elements of our projections are condensed, there should be some unconscious perception of a likeness, a reverse correspondence that binds us together while alienating us. (Volkan, 1988, 99, as quoted in Murer, 1999, 16)

Volkan's discussions of projection and dehumanization are important for our understanding of the other. However, some of the basic premises on which his arguments rest are problematic. His analogy of canvas tents is interesting, but it has the problem of providing an picture of boundedness, of inside-out perceptions, rather than identity as an open contestable concept. As a description of how categories are imagined as essentialized bodies his analogy is, however, relevant. As such it can be compared to Erikson's notion of totalism. His use of the term "ethnic" to describe such tents is more problematic, as identity is far from being confined to "ethnicity." As Erikson's work has shown, identity refers to a broad variety of psychological, cultural, and structural compositions. To this can be added the problems involved in Volkan's description of personal identity as a core identity that humans can lose, rather than as the incapacity to find a balance between identity and identity confusion as in Erikson's work. Finally there is the entire issue of object-relations theory, which treats the other as an object. Erikson was clearly distressed by British academics' embrace of Melanie Klein's object-relations theory as he rejected the idea that identity was set in early childhood at the same time as the term object applied to humans appalled him (THES Editorial, 2001).

Volkan is not entirely clear on this issue, however, as he repeatedly implies that the idea of the enemy is intrapsychic. He argues, for instance, that the closer the resemblance between the self and the other, the more likely the other is to become a suitable target for projection.

> First, although the groups may seem alike, they have minor differences. Second, rituals to maintain these major differences keep a psychological gulf between the opposing groups from killing one another. Attack only comes when playful ritualization of the preoccupation with minor differences is no longer maintained. (Volkan, 1988, 102, as quoted in Murer, 1999, 17)

Still, by suggesting that neighbors *are* different and that they easily make targets for externalization, Volkan seems to infer that the enemy-other *already* exists and *is* different from the self (Murer, 1999). This implies an essentialist, rather than a more relational and constructivist, view of self and other.

Volkan may not intend such a reading, but his continued use of object-relations theory, with its concentration on mind development as being dependent on the mother-child relationship, has consequences for his reasoning. It becomes hard, for instance, to understand complex and multiple identity formation in regard to interpersonal understanding and tolerance. Intimacy is for Erikson a fundamental part of identity construction. Understanding the other as object does little for explaining the conflicting nature of balancing intimacy and separateness as self is created in relation to others. Or as Murer (1999, 17) has asked, "Is it possible, for instance, to experience non-object related bonding, desire or other feelings such as guilt, hate or love towards the other?" Also, object-relations theory has difficulties in explaining what Lifton (1991) has called "doubling," namely that people can have human elements even though they can have the most evil sorts of behavior on other occasions, in other contexts. Here it is important to differentiate between the process of objectifying the other, and thus the self, in the search for a stable identity, and that of seeing the other as an already existing object.

Kristeva's treatment of self and others seems to respond to some of the problems involved in object-relations theory as she moves away from the subject-object dichotomy. Proceeding from Lacanian analysis, she sees the creation of self as an internal psychological process that rests not on the opposition I/Other, Inside/Outside, but rather on its combination. There is no deep or primary causality between the two. Instead they correspond to each other (Kristeva, 1982, 7, 66–67). She suggests that the antidote to xenophobia, racism, and the marginalization of others is to recognize the "foreigner within us" (Kristeva, 1991, 191). "He is the hidden face of our identity, the space that wrecks our abode, the time in which understanding and affinity founder. By recognizing him within ourselves, we are spared detesting him in himself" (Kristeva, 1991, 1). The other exists in our minds through imagination even when that other is not physically present. The fact that anti immigration feelings are sometimes stronger in places with few or no immigrants is an indication of such power of imagination. The clash with the other, "the identification of the self with that good or bad other that transgresses the fragile boundaries of the uncertain self, would thus be the source of an uncanny strangeness whose excessive features . . . cannot hide its permanent presence" (Kristeva, 1991, 189).

The important point here is that the enemy-other is not only created by the self, but previously has been part of the self (Murer, 1999). It becomes the *abject*, which differs from Volkan's object. "Abject. It is something rejected from which one does not part, from which one does not protect oneself as from an object" (Kristeva, 1982, 4). It is a combination of judgment and affect, of condemnation and yearning, of signs and drives. What causes abjection is that which disturbs identity, system or order. Economic crises, migration or other structural marginalization processes can, in other words, create abjection. Abject becomes a major ingredient of collective identity formation when the familiar "stranger" is suddenly recognized as a threat. It is at this point the other is no longer being circumscribed, reasoned with, or thrown aside. Instead, it becomes rejected and separated from the self, it appears as abject. "Arguments, demonstrations, proofs, etc.—the very logic of the symbolic—must conform to" this abjection (Kristeva, 1982, 15). In this way, the other created through abjection only exists as a mental representation of the subject. Those traits not wanted in the self are projected onto the other, implying that the differences are *perceived* by the self (not actually existing in an objective sense as Volkan argues), and are as intrapsychically created as the group-other itself (Murer, 1999).

The case of India can be used to illustrate Kristeva's discussion. Before the storming of the Golden Temple in 1984, the Sikhs and Hindus did not, as a general rule, see each other as enemies. They were parts of the same group self. Similarly the Hindus and Muslims had a more uncomplicated relationship before becoming part of the British colonized self, as well as prior to the partition in 1947 (the creation of Pakistan) (Kinnvall, 2002b). This adds weight to Kristeva's argument that in the process of splitting some aspects are valued and become integral to the newly constructed self, while others become devalued and externalized. Those aspects perceived as strange and alien within the newly constructed other seem uncomfortably familiar because it is the self repressed. However, the fear of the return of the repressed abject makes it essential to classify it as foreign as it otherwise would destroy the new subjective self and jeopardize the newly reestablished collective identity. A process of self-deception takes place to convince oneself that the abject has never been part of the self (Kristeva, 1991, 184; Murer, 1999, 18–19).

This is where debasement comes in. The self can only be guaranteed essential difference by systematically debasing the other in confrontation. Without such systematic debasement of the other, says Kristeva (1991, 187):

> whom I reject and with whom I identify, I lose my boundaries, I no longer have a container, the memory of experiences when I had been abandoned overwhelm me, I lose my composure. I feel "lost," "indistinct," "hazy."

Through debasement fear and desire are connected. By reducing the other to inhumanity, any required act to maintain the boundaries of self and other can be justified and hatred becomes an integrated part of the new definition of the self (Murer, 1999, 27).

This is similar to Volkan's discussion of projection and dehumanization. In comparison to Kristeva, however, Volkan finds his explanations in childhood development. He argues that when members of a group regress in the face of stressful conditions (disturbances, rapid changes, trauma), they come close to experiencing their enemy as the original reservoir of unintegrated bad parts of their childhood selves. These reservoirs often contain nonhuman objects, such as a pig for a Muslim child or the turban for a Christian child. In the same manner, adults, when regressed, tend to reactivate a sense of experiencing the enemy as nonhuman by attaching symbols to enemy images, symbols originally evolved in childhood. So, for example, when children learn to appreciate cleanliness, they disown, psychologically speaking, their own waste and begin to see it as dirty. This is similar to how groups, through essentialization of the other, often perceive the enemy as dirty. When, for instance, "one group insists that the other has a darker color, smells bad, or does dirty deeds, they are rejecting the other as if they were feces" (Volkan, 1997, 113).

Within this process prejudice is used as a means to differentiate one group from the other (similar to Kristeva's use of arguments and proofs as following upon abjection), and in order to retain their group identity. Rituals that foster such prejudice, ethnic jokes for instance, are effective in psychologically securing group identity. Often dehumanization is done in stages, where the enemy is first demonized but retains some qualities, while later he or she may be rendered as vermin and completely dehumanized. In the case of Rwanda, for instance, Tutsi were initially referred to as evil, but later this changed into *cafards*, meaning cockroaches. Hurting or killing cockroaches induce less guilt than killing humans would do (Volkan, 1997, 113).

In Kristeva's terminology dehumanization occurs as the collective image of the self becomes so ambiguous and devastating that the self engages in abjection. "I expel *myself*, I spit *myself* out, I abject *myself* with the same motion through which 'I' claim to establish *myself*" (Kristeva, 1982, 3, her emphasis). The other is viewed with spite, as a corpse, a worthless nonhuman. Hate, as argued by Murer (1999, 27), can thus construct a link between the present, the future and a re-created past. In this sense it serves as a social chain for successive generations as a particular event or trauma becomes mythologized and intertwined with a group's sense of self.

This is what Volkan (1997, 36–50), refers to as a "Chosen Trauma." A Chosen Trauma is often used to interpret new traumas. Thus it relies on previously experienced (real or imagined) rage and humiliation associated with victimization in the case of the Chosen Trauma, which is validated in a new context. As observed by Murer (1999), it is this process which often leads casual observers to conclude that ethnic conflicts may be timeless. Humans, Volkans argue, cannot accept change without mourning what is lost. We can mourn loved ones, or possessions, but we can "also mourn the loss of persons or things that we hate since hate, like love, connects us deeply to each other" (Volkan, 1997, 36). When no mourning process occurs, the result is often a long-term persistence of hurt feeling, which may result in despair and psychological breakdown.

In cases when loss or death remain insufficiently mourned, the mourner identifies indiscriminately with the dead, taking in both the loved and the hated aspects, wanting simultaneously to keep and destroy the image of the deceased. Often the perennial mourner lives symbolically in the life of the dead using linking objects (such as a favorite toy of a dead child) to remain in contact with the dead. Volkan (1997, 36–49) argues that, like individuals, large groups also mourn. The influence of a specific trauma or a severe and humiliating calamity that affects a large group forges a link between the psychology of the individual and that of the group. After such an event, mental images and stories begin to unfold as shared feelings, perceptions, fantasies, and interpretations of the event take place. Included in this process are mental defenses against painful or unacceptable feelings and thoughts. When such mental representations remain unresolved and continue to be experienced as persistent humiliation they are likely to affect the members of the group negatively. They become perennial mourners and as such their traumatized self-images are passed down to later generations in the hope that others may be able to mourn and resolve what the prior generation could not.

These images make up what Volkan refers to as the transmitted "psychological DNA" of the younger generation through its relationship with the former one. The use of DNA is somewhat unfortunate as it conjures up images of genetic inheritance. Thus, to avoid an essentialist reading of Volkan it is important to remember that what is transmitted is changing within the process of transmission. Chosen Traumas (and their opposite, Chosen Glories) provide the linking objects for later generations to be rediscovered, reinterpreted, and reused. Memories of a past trauma may lay dormant for generations only to be rediscovered as a collectivity experiences a new or secondary trauma. A political leader may for instance reignite a dormant group memory by reactivating the original trauma or glory (Volkan, 1997, 46). The case of India can once again be used for exemplification. Hindu nationalist leaders have, for instance, repeatedly invoked the partition to justify recent violent actions and to dehumanize the Muslim minority. The destruction of the Babri mosque by Hindu nationalists in 1992, the Kargil conflict in 1999, and the recent riots in Gujarat all provide ample examples of this (Kinnvall, 2002b). Partition has thus worked as a Chosen Trauma that is constantly referred to and validated in new contexts.

This second trauma may actually have little to do with the Chosen Trauma. However, the self is likely to defend against recent loss by perceiving it as continued oppression by the original "victimizing" enemy-other. The linking cycle can be found in the repeated usage of the abject-other created during the Chosen Trauma as it allows the younger generation to experience the pain and the loss of their elders. Also, as argued by Murer (1999, 30), "By expanding the Chosen Trauma to include losses associated with a secondary trauma, the group self 'reinvents' the previously ascribed abject with the traits necessary to be applicable in the new case. The 'old' enemy-other is, therefore responsible for 'new' losses."

Revisiting Erik Erikson: Group Conflict and Global/Local Disorders

Both Kristeva and Volkan give psychological explanations for group conflict. As such they inevitably draw parallels between the psychological makeup of the individual and that of the group. As a consequence they could, similar to Erikson, be accused of reductionism. However, this underplays the extent to which we can gain an understanding of group conflict by analyzing the group "as if" it is behaving similar to an individual whose own (constructed) definition of her social self suddenly feels threatened by traumatic events. Keeping the subject alive enables us to study the making of the "self" out of a plethora of context-specific "identities." At the level of practice, it allows us to tell stories of self. Furthermore, "the other" may be specific human collectives, which may commit **acts** like giving recognition. Crucially, inasmuch as they are seen as **acting**, their acts may also change" (Neumann, 1997, 20, bold text in original).

Second, there is a tendency in much social science literature on identity of not providing any psychological explanations at all out of fear of such reductionism. It is true that in isolation Volkan's and Kristeva's accounts may be lacking in deeper structural explanation. However, they add a crucial structural-psychological dimension that is all too often neglected in work on identity, nationalism, and group conflict. The social is never separated from the individual. As Erikson has argued,

> the outerworld of the ego is made up of the egos of others significant to it. They are significant because on many levels of crude or subtle communication, my whole being perceives in them a hospitality to the way they order their world and include me—a mutual affirmation, then, which can be depended upon to activate my being as I can be depended upon to activate theirs. (Erikson, 1968, 219)

What Kristeva and Volkan show in their different interpretations is how feelings of "ancient hatred" are constructed and maintained. These are not, as today's mass media often makes them out to be, primordial feelings of hatred or entrenched animosities waiting to break out in a largely chaotic world. Even critical scholars like Barber (1996), who disputes the historical fatalism of such discourses, still buys into them by talking about the "retribalization of the world." When, for example, a Croatian militiaman stitches an Ustache symbol to his uniform, he is doing more than acting out a preordained history or exercising a pregiven subjectivity. He is reproducing and rearticulating a historical representation (a Chosen Trauma) as a means to constitute his present subjective and collective identity—his social self (see Campbell, 1996, 174). Both Volkan's and Kristeva's texts are attempts to explain the psychological makeup that gives rise to such Chosen Traumas. The reexamination of identity theory in a socio-psychological light thus suggests that,

> the barriers between groups are at least partly constructed out of a process of projection. As many writers have argued, these projective mechanisms extrude unacceptable or ambivalently regarded aspects of the self or group and attribute them to an external or collective other. (Wurgaft, 1995, 71)

Erikson's discussion of pseudo-speciation refers to this vengeful phenomenon through which individuals narrow their definition of themselves to encompass only one particular group invested with meaning of an almost sacred intensity. In the name of the group, people become willing to discriminate, dehumanize, and even kill, sometimes over seemingly minor differences. Erikson's pseudo-speciation concept is particularly relevant today, as we see how people who have sometimes lived side by side become engaged in local conflict as a response to structural inequalities and global anxieties. Totalism, as Erikson defined it, is only another way of describing how identity in times of crisis tends to become essentialized. Totalism takes the form of essential categories and acts as a common ground from which to launch discriminatory, racist, and sexist politics. Descriptions of Sikhs as warriors, of Hindus as tolerant, or of Muslims as fanatic are all essentialist narratives that mainly serve as common unifiers for racist, exclusive constructions of the other. In the name of multiculturalism, such essentialist categories often becomes permanent.

In this limited sense, multiculturalism takes the form of neoracism (Volkan, 1997) which, compared to traditional racism is grounded not in biology but in anthropology and in an ideological commitment to the virtues of difference. Racist ideology, as a 1992 United Nations report observed:

> emphasizes the unique nature of the language, religions, mental and social structures, and value systems of immigrants of African, Arab, or Asian origin, for instance, in order to justify the need to keep human communities separate. It even goes so far as to contend that preserving their identity is in the interest of the communities concerned. By asserting a radical cultural pluralism, the new racism based on cultural differences tries, paradoxically, to look like genuine anti-racism and to show respect for all group identities. (quoted in Volkan, 1997, 22)

The policy of "multiculturalism" is hence consistent with the liberal emphasis on tolerance and the right to self-assertion and recognition of *the* group's (often perceived as inherited) identity (van Dijk, 1997; Tamir, 1999). Such a notion of "multiculturalism" reinforces assumptions of universality and individualism by giving the group homogenous universal features based on self-rights for the group. As a consequence it disregards unequal power distribution both between and within groups, globally as well as locally. In this sense it combines, as Zygmunt Bauman (2001, 135) has noted, the right to be different with the right to indifference, thus justifying status quo and current structures of power. The migratory-based segregation of people, schools, and workplaces in many urban cities is a reflection of such transformations.

Erikson's work provides a foundation for appreciating the influence of such broader social factors on human (in)security as it goes beyond the child-rearing experiences to account for social, structural, and cultural factors in shaping personality. It thus provides a psychological account for understanding neo-racism as yet another form of pseudo-speciation. At the same time it clarifies how a lack of stable ideologies and values may create an atmosphere of disillusionment and cynicism that contributes to feelings of emptiness and meaninglessness. To see this as a process that stretches far beyond childhood experiences is more fruitful for understanding identity conflict than is the search for linear relationships between early childhood events and later developments—a tendency that characterizes much contemporary psychoanalytic theory (Eagle, 1997).

The strife for unity is thus manifest in a wish to experience a feeling of "wholeness"—to become a product, a total category. It does not mean, however, that such unity is essential or primordial. Instead, when Giddens (1991) argues that human beings are concerned with existential questions of being, such as *existence itself*, the relations between the *external world and human life*, the *existence of other persons*, and *self-identity*, he is careful to stress how such concerns emerge in situations of uncertainty and insecurity. Unequal power relationships, macrostructural changes, and other local effects of the global, are likely to result in a preoccupation with these questions as a means to increase ontological security and reduce existential anxiety. The other, being already an integrated part of one's self-definition, is then likely to assume a new existence. As Kristeva (1991, 13) has argued, "living with the other, with the foreigner, confronts us with the possibility or not of being an other."

Kristeva and Volkan are both concerned with the role of aggression in human beings, including how and why investment in emotionally bonded groups sometimes leads to mass violence and horrifying acts. By emphasizing the other as a mental image, an intrapsychic abject-other, onto which the self projects its (or the group's) unwanted traits we may escape the tendency to describe conflicts in essentialized terms. The emphasis on trauma also brings attention to the emotional aspects of human relatedness as it points to the need for ontological and existential security. The effects of globalization are pertinent in this respect as they display all the possible features of causing emotional traumas of alienation, loss of self-esteem, and images of lost objects such as territory.

Conclusion

Contemporary identity thus takes many forms and serves as both identification and differentiation markers, reflecting intimacy as well as separation. Identity, we have learnt from Erikson, is both historically constructed and context dependent. Such identities may be local, regional, national, global or a combination of these. Together they consist of those patterns of "nodal points" or nexuses between the global and the local. By emphasizing the global-local nexus, it is possible to conceive of the actual meeting of the two as a process, rather than seeing them as opposites or dichotomies. The concrete meeting is not between a self and an object-other who remains a passive acultural vector, but rather between two, both social and intrapsychic, constructions that become reconstituted through the actual interaction.

Within this encounter, constructed cultural attributes and Chosen Traumas provide not only the symbolic references or resources but they also provide for the revival of some or other aspects of a collective past. They can, in other words, act as a source of revivalism, fundamentalism, and national chauvinism. "The notions of self may generate conceptions of the superiority or inferiority of cultures and induce fears of the Other as posing a constant threat to the self" (Alam, 1999, 130). It is within this process that neat distinctions are created between concepts, such as modern and traditional, secular and religious, majority and minority, the national and the foreigner, the strong and the weak, and so on, even when in reality there are no such clear-cut boundaries.

However, global processes of liberalization, democratization, communication, technological changes, and the breakdown of hierarchical structures work to intensify the reification of such boundaries. As the global meets the local, as individuals and groups are confronted by these macrostructural challenges, the emotional appeal to one stable identity becomes the solution to feelings of ontological security and existential anxiety. It is here, to use Erikson's terminology, that the cultural and the social are linked with the psychological. It is at this level that power forms the subject and acts upon her in a constructive sense of the term. As argued by Judith Butler: "power works not merely to dominate or oppress existing subjects, but also to form subjects . . . the formative dimension of power is to be understood in a nonmechanistic and nonbehavioristic fashion" (Butler 1997, 18, quoted in Smith, 2000, 160–161).

Erikson's discussion of social selves, generativity, and pseudospeciation provides us with such a nonmechanistic and nonbehavioristic foundation from which to understand not only why group conflict takes place, but also how conflict can be prevented. Hence his continued insistence on the impossibility of separating family and work, public and private, and intimacy and separation constitutes a way to give due attention to real structural inequalities as they are affecting real people. Also, emphasizing the relational aspects of identity formation and identity change provides a real possibility of not only accepting the other, but of being in her place, which means "imagine and make oneself other for oneself" (Kristeva, 1991, 13).

Erikson's account of Gandhi (1969) and the potential of nonviolent action is an attempt in that direction. In this he argues that "man perishes from senseless instinctual needs" and that therefore Gandhi's awareness is essential to the future of human beings. Whether men or women have such instincts can of course be debated and Erikson does not answer the question of what we will do in instances when nonviolent protest is repressed or when taking up arms provide better results than non-violent action for marginalized groups (Lipsitz and Kritzer, 1975). What he does do, however, is to stress the need for inclusive identities and mutuality even though he does not give any clear answers as to how we can obtain such nonessentialist identities.

However, an important starting point must be to unmask those hidden power structures involved in the appeal to one and only one inclusionary identity. Erikson's work highlights how such structures can be contextually understood and made sense of at a cultural-psychological level. Volkan and Kristeva take his work one step further as they explore, in different ways, the structural-psychological compositions of group conflicts. Their focus on strangers, neoracism, and Chosen Traumas all have a strong structural component. And their emphasis on the importance of positive changes in economy and structure to achieve peaceful coexistence between individuals and groups, accentuates the need to grasp insecurity as both a structural and a psychological process. Recognizing and dealing with the real structural insecurities for many people as they are having to learn to cope in an increasingly complex and globalized world, must be the only viable alternative for achieving such coexistence.

Notes

1. For general accounts of globalization, see Baylis and Smith, 2002; Held and McGrew, 1999. For more skeptical accounts, see Hirst and Thompson, 1996; Scott, 1997. For more critical accounts, see Kellner in Axtmann, 1998; Scholte, 2000; Appadurai, 1993; King, 1997. For the relationship between modernity and globalization see Giddens, 1990; Alam, 1999; Bauman, 2001; Hall, 1992; and Hoogvelt, 2001. For a more in-depth analysis of the main argument of this article with a specific focus on India, see Kinnvall, forthcoming.

2. Here is should be noted that the breakdown of such structures may also create opportunities for many as they can be both hierarchical and patriarchal as well as repressive in other ways.

3. In this regard, it is interesting to note that his main biographer, Lawrence J. Friedman (1999), calls him an incipient postmodernist.

References

Alam, J. *India: Living with Modernity*. Delhi: Oxford University Press, 1999.

Appadurai, A. "Disjuncture and Difference in the Global Cultural Economy," in P. Williams and L. Chrisman (eds.), *Colonial Discourse and Post-Colonial Theory*. London: Harvester Wheatsheaf, 1993.

Axtman, R. *Globalization and Europe*. London: Pinter, 1998.

Barber, B. *Jihad vs. McWorld*. New York: Ballantine Books, 1996.

Bauman, Z. *Globalization: The Human Condition*. Oxford: Polity Press, 1998.

Bauman, Z. *Community: Seeking Safety in an Insecure World*. Cambridge: Polity Press, 2001.

Baylis, J., and S. Smith. *The Globalization of Politics*. Oxford: Oxford University Press, 2002.

Brenman-Gibson, M. "The Legacy of Erik Homburger Erikson," *Psychoanalytic Review* 84, no.3 (June 1997): 330–35.

Calhoun, C. (ed.). *Social Theory and the Politics of Identity*. Cambridge: Blackwell Publishers, 1994.

Campbell, D., "Violent Performances: Identity, Sovereignty, Responsibility," in Lapid and Kratochvil (eds.). *The Return of Culture and Identity in International Relations Theory*. Boulder, Lynne Rienner, 1996.

———. *Critical Social Theory*. Oxford, Blackwell Publishers, 1995.

Castles, S., and A. Davidson. *Citizenship and Migration: Globalization and the Politics of Belonging*. New York: Routledge, 2000.

Dannefer, D. "Adult Development and Social Theory: A Paradigmatic Reappraisal," *American Sociological Review* 49, no. 1 (February, 1984): 100–116.

Eagle, M. "Contributions of Erik Erikson," *Psychoanalytic Review* 84, no. 3 (June 1997): 337–47.

Erikson, E. *Childhood and Society*. New York: Norton, 1950.

———. "Identity and the Life Cycle," *Psychological Issues* 1. New York: International Universities Press, 1959.

———. *Identity, Youth and Crisis*. New Yaork: Norton, 1968.

———. *Gandhi's Truth: On the Origins of Militant Nonviolence*. New York: Norton, 1969.

———. *The Life Cycle Completed: A Review*. New York: Norton, 1982.

Friedman, L. J. *Identity's Architect: A Biography of Erik Erikson*. New York: Scribner, 1999.

Gergen K. *An Invitation to Social Construction*. London: Sage, 1999.

Giddens, A. *The Consequences of Modernity*. Stanford, CA: Stanford University Press, 1990.

———. *Modernity and Self-identity: Self and Society in the Late Modern Age*. Cambridge, England: Polity Press, 1991.

Gilligan, C. *In a Different Voice: Psychological Theory and Women's Development*. Cambridge. MA: Harvard University Press, 1982.

Hall, S. (ed.), *Modernity and Its Futures*. London: Polity Press, 1992.

Harvey, D. *The Condition of Postmodernity*. Cambridge: Blackwell, 1989.

―――. "From Space to Place and Back Again: Reflections on the Conditions of Postmodernity," in J. Bird et al. (eds.), *Mapping the Futures: Local Culture, Global Change.* London: Routledge, 1993, pp.3–29.

Held, D. and A. McGrew. *Global Transformations.* Stanford, CA: Stanford University Press, 1999.

Hirst, P., and G. Thompson. *Globalization in Question.* Cambridge, England: Polity Press, 1996.

Hoogvelt, A. *Globalization and the Postcolonial World: The New Political Economy of Development.* Basingstoke, England: Palgrave, 2001.

Horst, E. "Reexamining Gender Issues in Erikson's Stages of Identity and Intimacy," *Journal of Counseling & Development* 73 (January/February, 1995): 271–78.

Hurrell, A., and N. Woods. (eds.). *Inequality, Globalization, and World Politics.* Oxford: Oxford University Press, 1999.

King, Anthony, ed., *Culture, Globalization and the World-System: Contemporary Conditions for the Representation of Identity,* Minneapolis: MN, University of Minnesota Press, 1997.

Kinnvall, C. "Analyzing the Global-Local Nexus," in *Globalization and Democratization in Asia: The Construction of Identity,* C. Kinnvall and K. Jönsson (eds.). London: Routledge, 2002a.

―――. "Nationalism, Religion and the Search for Chosen Traumas: Comparing Sikh and Hindu Identity Construction," *Ethnicities* 2, no. 1 (2002b): 79–106.

―――. *Globalization and the Construction of Identity: Democracy, Diversity and Nationhood in India,* New Delhi & London, Sage (forthcoming).

Kolodner, E. "The Political Economy of the Rise and Fall of Hindu Nationalism," *Journal of Contemporary Asia* 25, no. 2 (1995).

Kovel, J. "Erik Erikson's Psychohistory," *Social Policy* (March/April, 1974): 60–64.

Kristeva, J. *Powers of Horror: An Essay of Abjection.* New York: Columbia University Press, 1982.

―――. *Strangers to Ourselves.* New York: Columbia University Press, 1991.

Lifton, R. J. "Erikson, Erik & Joan: Award Speeches." *Revision* 14, no. 2 (Fall 1991): 113–25.

Lipsitz, L. and H. M. Kritzer. "Unconventional Approaches to Conflict Resolution: Erikson and Sharp on Nonviolence," *The Journal of Conflict Resolution,* 19, no. 4 (December 1975): 713–33.

Mack, J. E. "Erikson, Erik and Joan – Award speeches," *Revision,* 14, no. 2 (Fall 1991): 113–25.

Manners, I. "Europe and the World: The Impact of Globalization," in *Contemporary Europe,* R. Sakwa and A. Stevens (eds.). Basingstoke, England: Palgrave, 2000.

Marcia, J. "Identity in Adolescence," in *Handbook of Adolescent Psychology,* J. Adelson (ed.). New York: Wiley, 1980.

McBride, M. "Autonomy and the Struggle for Female Identity: Implications for Counseling Women," *Journal of Counseling and Development* 69 (1990): 22–26.

McFadden, S. H. "Religion, Personality, and Aging: A Life Span Perspective," *Journal of Personality* 67: no. 6 (December 1999): 1081–1103.

136   *Kinnvall*

Murer, J. S. "New Approach to Understanding Nationalism and Ethnic Conflict: Adaptive Cultural Mourning," paper presented at the twenty-second Annual Conference of the International Society of Political Psychology, Amsterdam, July, 1999.

Neumann, Iver. "The Limits of Subject/Other Perspectives," paper presented at the International Studies Association conference, Toronto, March 18-22, 1997.

Ogilvie, D. M. and R. D. Ashmore. "Self-with-Other Representation as a Unit of Analysis in Self-Concept Research," in *The Relational Self*, R. Curtis (ed.). New York: Guildford Press, 1991, 282–313.

Ong, A. *Flexible Citizenship–The Cultural Logics of Transnationality*. Durham, NC: Duke University Press, 1999.

Orlovsky J. "Sex-role Orientation, Identity Formation, and Self-esteem in College Men and Women," *Sex Roles* 3 (1977): 561–75.

Pathak, A. *Indian Modernity: Contradictions, Paradoxes and Possibilities*. New Delhi: Gyan, 1998.

Robertson, R. *Globalization, Social Theory and Global Culture*. London, England: Sage, 1992.

Robins, R. S., and J. M. Post. *Political Paranoia: The Psychopolitics of Hatred*. New Haven, CT: Yale University Press, 1997.

Scholte J. A. *Globalization: A Critical Introduction*. Basingstoke: Macmillan, 2000.

Scott A. (ed.) *The Limits of Globalization*. London: Routledge, 1997.

Sigel, R. (ed.) *Political Learning in Adulthood*. Chicago: University of Chicago Press, 1989.

Simai, M. "The Politics and Economics of Global Employment," in *Global Employment: An International Investigation into the Future of Work*, vol. 1, M. Simai (ed.). London: Zed, 1995.

Smith, A. "The Sacred Dimension of Nationalism," *Millennium: Journal of International Studies* 29, no. 3 (2000): 71–81

Smith, T. "Social Violence and Conservative Social Psychology: The Case of Erik Erikson," *Journal of Peace Research* 13, no. 1 (1976): 1–12.

Tamir, Yael. "Siding with the Underdogs," in *Is Multiculturalism Bad for Women?* Susan Okin (ed.). Princeton, NJ: Princeton University Press, 1999.

Times Higher Education Supplement (THES) Editorial, "Why I Believe Psychohistory Should Acknowledge Its Founding Father," *The Times Higher Education Supplement*, March 16, 2001.

van Dijk, T. "Political Discourse and Racism: Describing Others in Western Parliaments," in *The Language and Politics of Exclusion: Others in Discourse*, H. Riggins (ed.). London, Sage, 1997.

Volkan, V. *The Need to Have Enemies and Allies: From Clinical Practice to International Relationships*. Northvale, NJ: Jason Aronson, 1988.

Volkan, V. *Bloodlines: From Ethnic Pride to Ethnic Terrorism*. Boulder, CO: Westview Press, 1997.

Weiland, S. "Erik Erikson: Ages, Stages and Stories," *Generations* 93, no. 2 (Spring/Summer, 1993): 17–23.

Wurgaft, L. D. "Identity in World History: A Postmodern Perspective," *History & Theory* 34, no. 2 (1995): 67–86.

Chapter Nine

Religion and Identity: Deciphering the Construals of Islamic Fundamentalism

Lina Haddad Kreidie

The September 11 attacks on New York and Washington, D.C. represent the most audacious expression to date of the fundamentalist Islamic hatred for the West, in general, and the United States, in particular. In an era of globalization and trends calling for more interdependence and cooperation, Islamic fundamentalism, a particularistic movement, is viewed as a wind against the trends of integration. However, Islamism is not a new phenomenon, though the term fundamentalism is. Throughout different historical eras, Islamic revival and resurgence evolved with different emerging movements which either opposed the Islamic beliefs and/or presented other sociopolitical alternatives which contradicted the comprehensive characteristic of Islam.[1] Fundamentalism, a Protestant categorization of those following the Bible literally, has been used to categorize Muslims who follow the Qur'an and *Sharia* faithfully to the word. For simplicity, I will use the term fundamentalists for Muslims in this way: for those who follow the Qur'an and the *Sharia* literally.

Indeed there are real reasons, real grievances, for why our world is in such turmoil and danger today. There are real and serious reasons young people in certain parts of the world are choosing to become what many Westerners call terrorists and what they themselves call martyrs and freedom fighters. However, in this study, I will not delve into these issues but I will try and answer the question of why Western policy makers fail in dealing with Islamic fundamentalist groups. Is it the now-synonymous association of fundamentalism with terrorism, or does it have to do with uniquely cultural differences or, indeed, the clash of civilizations?

The belief system of Islamic fundamentalists reflects an overlap between personal ethics, social mores, and governmental rules. Governments that wish to deal successfully with the increasingly important Islamic groups in or out of government need to recognize and understand this cognitive framework. Failure to do so will result in a conceptual skewing of Islamic fundamentalism that reflects a Western, rationalist mode of thinking which is fused by ethnocentricity, prejudice, and a biased political science technical lexicon which fails to describe accurately the dynamics of what is taking place in another cultural setting.[2]

Much of the literature pertaining to Islamic fundamentalism illustrates the disparate explanations that various theorists have offered for the resurgence, behavior, and attitudes of Islamic fundamentalists.[3] Rational choice theorists reject the idea of fundamentalism in general as pathological, contending that fundamentalism is a commodity provided by religious institutions which function in perfectly competitive markets with nil costs and excess profit. Iannaccone, for one, claims that people are analogous to consumers and approach religion in the same way they approach other objects or commodities of choice: they evaluate costs and benefits of religion to maximize their net benefits.[4] Limited by its inability to comprehend cognitive differences and psychological motivations that trump economic and political motivations for behavior, this Western rationalist perspective leads to a distorted image of fundamentalist groups and hence provides both practitioners and researchers with few tools and strategies to understand and predict the potential effects of these groups on domestic, regional, and international stability.

Other traditional theoretical frameworks fail to sufficiently explain the impetus that drives an individual to convert to fundamentalism largely because such theories often overlook the critical components of the religious doctrine itself in deciphering the decisive factors that drive or constrain the actions of Islamic fundamentalists. Some see conversion to Islamic fundamentalism as a reaction to rapid social change and economic and political Instability.[5] Belief system analysts view Islamic fundamentalists as revivalists[6] or reformists of ancient Islamic thought[7] and/or modern radicals.[8]

This critique of traditional approaches also suggests the need to understand the cognitive perceptual structure of fundamentalists and in particular to ask how identity constrains or precedes choices and thus shapes the behavior of religious fundamentalists.   To make this argument, I treat Islamic fundamentalism as a form of ethical-political behavior that can best be explained through a social-psychological approach. I focus on *identity* and on how fundamentalists construe and interpret the reality they see around them. Emphasizing identity, I expand on previous work with Kristin Renwick Monroe to suggest Islamic fundamentalism attracts because it provides a basic identity, an identity which in turn provides the foundation of daily living.[9] We can best understand the fundamentalist perspective through reference to a worldview that makes no distinction between public and private, in which truth is revealed by revelation, and reason is subservient to religious doctrine. Religious dictates dominate all basic issues, and only within the confines of the fundamentalist identity are choices decided by cost/benefit calculus.[10]

The Islamic Fundamentalists' Identity

To probe the nature of Islamic fundamentalist identity, I offer an analysis of the interviews I conducted with twenty self-proclaimed Islamic fundamentalists and contrast these to my interviews with five Islamic non-fundamentalists. My intention is to differentiate moderate to secular Muslims for whom Islam is a religion in the same sense that Christianity is a religion for many in the West, and from those for whom Islam takes on a more fundamental meaning. As a way of sharpening the focus, I deal particularly with those who have converted to Islam from other beliefs since their commitment tends to be the most intense. What makes them follow and abide strictly by those beliefs and ideologies, and what drives or constrains their action thereafter?

Interviewees were placed on a religious continuum from left to right as follows: Secular was defined as those who inherit their religion from their parents but do not follow its laws and rituals. These people might believe in some Islamic principles but do not consider themselves to be true Muslim believers. Good Muslims believe that Islam is a good religion and accept most of its doctrines, but abide by few of its rituals such as celebrating the feasts or following the hereditary laws and marriage customs. Orthodox Muslims follow the five pillars of Islam, live by the laws and regulations of Islam, the *Sharia*, and try to apply it in most aspects of life, but do not follow these mandates strictly; such individuals might compromise some of Islamic practices such as the dress code and banking with interest. Islamic fundamentalists are Muslims who follow the Qur'an and the *Sharia* strictly and literally in all aspects of life. Nonfundamentalists located themselves between secular and orthodox; Islamic fundamentalists located themselves on the right of this.

I will be relying on a political psychology approach focusing on identity and the importance of cognitive construals (interpretations and perceptions) in explaining political behavior.[11] I am interested in constructing a model for how Islamic fundamentalists view themselves in relation to others—which I will argue is not based on concepts of utility or self-interest. To better understand an Islamic fundamentalist cognitive framework, we need to utilize a cognitive perceptual theory that elucidates an individual's beliefs about how the world works and shows how that individual organizes and makes sense of reality at any particular time.[12]

I believe that Islam provides a social identity for fundamentalists from which ancillary identities and construals are derived. Contrary to rationalist explanations of fundamentalist behavior, it is not utility that motivates action but rather the defense of the perceived Islamic identity that overwhelms other acquired identities. Western psychology today is saturated with the post-Enlightenment idea that individuals act out of self-interest and make calculated goal-oriented decisions based on a cost-benefit analysis, yet this account seems to fail thoroughly in offering a compelling explanation for the behavior of Islamic fundamentalists. How can this rational actor approach explain the behavior of people when the line between private and public fades, moral obligations supersede private interests, and the self is sacrificed to promote God's word?

The present chapter builds on my earlier joint work with Monroe comparing the worldviews of fundamentalist with nonfundamentalist Muslims.[13] The theoretical model we have developed to explain perceptual psychological similarities among fundamentalists we term the cognitive perceptual approach.[14] The cognitive-perceptual approach considers the behavior of Islamic fundamentalists in terms of ethical-political and identity-driven, rather than cost-benefit calculated, behavior. Utilizing a narrative and survey interview technique, Monroe and I found that Islamic fundamentalism attracts because it provides a basic identity, an identity which in turn provides the foundation of daily living. The fundamentalist perspective itself is best understood through reference to a worldview that makes no distinction between public and private, in which truth is revealed by revelation, and reason is subservient to religious doctrine.[15]

In this study, I go one step beyond our former work and suggest that though the actions of all the interviewees are to some degree motivated by identity-driven interest, the choices made by the nonfundamentalists are driven more by utility—which seems to be an element lacking in the choice to convert by the Islamic fundamentalist interviewees. The primary differences I perceive are the following: (1) the faith of the fundamentalist provides an overarching and basic identity that shapes all other ancillary identities such as being a mother, a student, or a leader; (2) the choice of conversion to Islamic fundamentalism is not a calculated one: for the Islamic fundamentalist it is a necessity in terms of fulfilling his/her individual identity (i.e., being true to oneself); and (3) the way Islamic fundamentalists perceive reality reflects a comprehensive worldview in which personal ethics, social mores, and political ideologies overlap to form one coherent and inseparable system of thought in which reason is subservient to faith, the individual is secondary to the Islamic community and the mandates of Allah's law, and science and technology are a means of affirming God's perfection. There does not seem to be any doubt in the minds of the fundamentalist interviewees that Islam sets their mode of action: the Qur'an and Islamic teachings establish the responsibilities of a mother, a worker, a leader, a fighter, etc., and a true Muslim follows these mandates of God. Um Sajed endorses this idea that I found common to each fundamentalist interviewee: "Islam dominates all aspects of life. Islam dictates my role as a wife, a mother, and a social worker." Suzzane echoes Um Sajed's assertion: "I raise my kids, and I deal with my husband, my family, and my friends according to Islam. Why should I do otherwise? I find the answer for everything in Islam."

Through my interviews with Islamic fundamentalists, it has become evident to me that their actions are defined by an identity which is intricately tied with and in many ways inseparable from their religiosity, that is, Islam, which supercedes all other self-concepts including national identity, familial ties, or any other single determinate. Susan emphasizes, "I am a Muslim first, then I am a national of whatever country I am in." Ziad adds, "What I like about this country [the United States] is that all of us in the youth group at the mosque, whether Jordanian, Lebanese, Iraqi, we all identify as Muslims. We are Muslims first." Interestingly, I found that these conversions are not a phenomenon unique to fundamentalists living in the United States—what many scholars have called an identity crisis of those lost between two different cultures. The Islamic identity overarches other identities, even among those living among their own people and in a similar cultural background. Imad who lives in Lebanon, unambiguously addresses this issue and refutes the notion of national identity: "I refuse to be identified as an Arab nationalist. I am a Muslim. This Arab nationalism is nothing but a Western plot to destroy Islam."

The Islamic identity goes beyond national borders; Islamic fundamentalist interviewees refused to be identified first with any nation-state. They belong to the Islamic *Umma* (nation) first and then to any other nationality that does not contradict their Islamic sense of self.

View of Self in Relation to Others

Islamic fundamentalists perceive their role in relation to others as that of an example of Islam. The way fundamentalists view themselves and portray their relationship to others is by declaring their difference and setting an example for those who are lost in darkness. When discussing the *hijab* May declares, "*I wear it and am proud of it. It makes me feel dis-*

tinguished from others" [emphasis added]. Aida who converted at age forty furthers this notion: "I wear the hijab because I want to declare that I am a Muslim; wherever I go I want everyone to know that I am a Muslim." This sentiment was manifested in a variety of ways in many of my interviews. Abdul is a thirty-nine-year-old Shiite, married with three children. Born and raised in Beirut by a rich liberal Muslim family, he attended a Christian Maronite private school. In his soul searching, Abdul decided to travel to Iran to obtain his religious education. His conversion to Islam made him lose his family's financial support but nevertheless he pursued his education in Islamic studies. He returned to Lebanon and joined the Hizbu'llah movement. He maintains a high-security position in the party. Abdul was very welcoming and willing to offer any information that will promote the Islamic image. He confirms, "I am proud of my way of life and I guess my friends from all denominations respect me more today." Ziad sees himself as a true believer with high morals. He explains that he was never able to identify with others because he finds them secular and immoral.

Nuha eloquently reiterates a sentiment common to each Islamic fundamentalist interviewee: "I am no longer in darkness. Islam enlightened my life. I see all others in darkness." For each Islamic fundamentalist that I have interviewed, Islam provides a sense of distinctiveness from others: they see themselves as the seers amid the blind and often choose to present the path to others by serving as an example, a testimony to the grace of Islam.

Cost Is Not an Issue!

Rational choice theorists argue that realizing a satisfying identity can itself be considered a form of self-interested behavior. The empirical evidence presented in this study suggests that to the extent to which these possibilities exist they are the unintended consequences of actions taken for reasons other than those that drive rational choice theories.[16]

From the interviews I conducted with the Islamic fundamentalists, three main ideas were common to all my interviewees: (1) their primary concern is to follow divine orders with sincere belief and no questioning; (2) they conceive themselves as fundamentalists who are concerned primarily with God and see themselves as an indivisible part of a bigger Islamic nation; and (3) contrary to rational choice theory, they do not view the world in terms of costs and benefits.

Often decisions to adhere to the codes of Islam in today's society are not easy and do not represent the product of a typical cost-benefit analysis. Accordingly, the decision to adhere to the Islamic dress code is not an easy one for many Islamic women. Though many of the women I interviewed reside in communities familiar with the *hijab*, they explain the initial discomfort with wearing the Islamic attire proscribed for woman. Soon, however, many claimed they began to feel it less a constraint and more an act of liberation. The *hijab* itself seems to some degree to represent a manifestation of their respective personal identity with Islam and as such, a process of weighing the costs and benefits of the *hijab* are no longer an intrinsic part of the thought process. Aida openly articulates the initial uneasiness she felt about other people's attitude toward her:

> To tell you the truth, the first few days, even months, I felt awkward wearing the long coat and *hijab*, and I used to avoid people's looks. But later I felt very comfortable and confident of my dress code. Dear, I am very lucky that I got this strength from Allah, and I would like other people to know that I am blessed with Allah's guidance. I wish that others would follow my way.

In addition to the actions and reactions that seem to fall outside the scope of what one might consider cost-benefit analysis, such as the ones mentioned in the foregoing paragraphs, the concepts of I, us, and we are juxtaposed to the notion of them or others: these differentiations are emphasized in all of the narratives with the Islamic fundamentalists. This further illustrates that the actions of Islamic fundamentalists are more often driven by an identity, a basic identity associated with Islam, that dominates all other identities and related interests.

Conversion Is Not a Choice among Alternatives

Consistently throughout my interviews with Islamic fundamentalists I found that these individuals, unlike my other interviewees, did not perceive decisions made in line with their beliefs as choices, but rather as a manifestation of their respective identities in line with the mandates of their Islamic faith. In response to my inquiry about the things that made the interviewees choose this way of life and how the decision to follow Islam affected their lives, Obeidi responded:

> I cannot say that there was a specific event or any influence from my family that might have shaped my decision. My interest in Islam just came naturally. As a Muslim, I follow Islam in its entirety and globality. As a Muslim, I should work on calling my friends and family to turn to Islam. I joined the Islamic group to serve Islam.

Nonfundamentalist View of Self

In contrast to fundamentalists, when asked to describe themselves, Islamic nonfundamentalists referred to various identities, none of which
were dictated primarily by their faith in Islam or their religiosity. Lama is
a thirty-two-year-old mother of two boys and a girl. Lama was raised in a
middle-class conservative Muslim family. She moved to the United States
with her husband in the late eighties. A wife with a degree in engineering,
Lama is not working now because she has two baby boys. She falls into
the category of a good Muslim, believes in the doctrines of Islam, and
performs most of the Islamic rituals. She says:

> I am a devoted mother and wife. I am not working now because
> I want to give my kids all the time needed. When they grow up
> and I am sure that they are on the right track, then I will pur-
> sue my career. Some might say that it will be too late. I disagree
> because now I am investing in my children. When they grow up
> and they turn out to be good guys, if Allah wills, then I will be
> proud of them, and this will be a reward for me.

The Islamic nonfundamentalists do not immediately identify themselves as Muslims. Omar identifies himself as a good citizen, Moe as an
engineer and father, and Faris as a student and as a good person. None of
them presented themselves as Muslims or appeared to imagine themselves as Muslims first, although later in the interviews each—except for
one, Omar[17]—described him- or herself as good Muslims. From my interviews with the four distinct groups, ranging from most to least fundamentalist, it appears that the further we move from fundamentalism, the
more variegated the identity.[18] An individual more to the right of the
spectrum tends to express more differentiated layers of connecting
particulars that form his or her identity, while to the left of the spectrum
where I have placed Islamic fundamentalists, the identity seems to be
more coherent, unified, and oriented toward an identification with Islam.
While Faris, a good to orthodox Muslim, primarily identifies himself as a
good student, he also views himself as an independent and dynamic person capable of making choices among which he cites *choosing* to be a
dedicated Muslim, though without what he sees to be social or situational
pressure. Immediately, we see a distinction between these attitudes that
encompasses the notion of choice and those of the Islamic fundamentalists, who identify themselves with Islam so thoroughly and necessarily
that it appears not to have been a choice, decision, or an act of will.
Omar, too, though on the other side of the continuum from Faris, pre-

sents himself as an amalgam of dynamic identities. He describes himself as a single father who performs his obligation toward his son Charles. He perceives himself as an honest and straightforward person both in private and at work, and as an ideal citizen.

Again, my interviews suggest that as we move down the continuum from fundamentalism toward secular, we find more overlapping identities and a worldview less influenced or developed by one's relation to their religion. We see that the Islamic fundamentalists' sense of self as defined by their faith in Islam supercedes all other identities: an identity so cohesive it appears to be virtually impossible to compromise.

Actions Are Identity, Not Utility, Driven

Within the context of Islamic life, cost/benefit calculation may and often is applied to a variety of quotidian considerations and choices, but it seems to play virtually no role in decisions and issues that touch upon the fundamentalist's sense of self, especially as measured by preestablished Islamic dictates. A good example of this principle is Rana, a U.S. citizen who became a convert. She is a mother of two boys, and a woman who comes from an upper-middle-class, secular Muslim family. Rana worked as an accountant in an American corporation which she later had to quit because of unyielding pressure she faced after she donned the *hijab*. Her husband is a physician and his professional life necessitates many social contacts in which wearing the *hijab* might cause an embarrassment to him. However, Rana is not willing to reverse her decision in response to her husband's numerous requests. It is exceedingly clear from her responses that the costs did not present a real obstacle to Rana in any decision that touches on her sense of self, and the possible benefits that could result from abandoning this identity and faith are not real perceived choices for her. When asked if her dress code conflicted with her lifestyle at work and among family and friends, Rana confidently answered:

> My husband asked me not to abide by the dress code because this might affect his business and eventually our life. But to tell you the truth, it was not a matter of choice to me. I did not care about his business meetings. I had an inner feeling, which I had to follow.

I wanted to find out whether a cost/benefit analysis eventually does come into the decision-making process once overlapping Islamic dictates come into play. I followed up her last response with this inquisitive question. "But Islam orders you to respect your husband and to follow his demands." Rana then responded:

> It is true that Islam asks us to follow the wish of our husbands, but it is true only when he is a true believer. No, if my husband knows better about Islam, he wouldn't have requested this. This was a decision from my inner self. I believe in what I am doing. I feel that this is me now.

Rana's clear and eloquent response once again portrays that the decisions made by most Islamic fundamentalists are not dependant on an individual cost/benefit weighing process, but rather an identity that is formed in line with the teachings of Islam. Similarly, for Nuha, the cost was not a question. She converted at age thirty-three, more than twenty-two years ago, and her son is today the leader of a fast-growing Islamic fundamentalist Sunnite group. Nuha expresses virtually the same rationale for her decision:

> [At first] my husband was not interested at all. I had to talk to him over and over again. It is not easy for me to disobey my husband. But I could not but do it. I decided to follow the Islamic doctrines. I followed them all, without exception. My husband later agreed with me. He then became a true Muslim.

When asked specifically about cost, Rana and Nuha reflected a way of thinking outside the realm of the rationalist's limited explanation of human reasoning and actions. Although they understood the concept of cost/benefit calculation, and understood the huge costs associated with their conversion in terms of family disapproval, relationship with friends, and/or for their respective career choices, none of these issues represented a deterrent to their decision to convert or to subsequent decisions about their lives. What might seem to be necessary considerations to the average Westerner (i.e., keeping a job or maintaining a family relationship) were not essential to the decision to convert for Islamic fundamentalists. When asked about benefits of conversion and adhering to the Islamic way of life, Islamic fundamentalist interviewees did not consider any social, material, or psychological benefit in making their decision to convert, but rather expressed their decision as a mandate from without, a destiny which they fulfilled untouched by the enticement of reward. For example, both Nuha and Rana recognized the disapproval of family, friends, and/or coworkers to their conversion and way of life, yet were unwilling to alter their external actions in the least to mitigate daily situations. Rana tells of her tribulations in the workplace:

> My *hijab* was a surprise to my boss and other employees in the accounting corporation I worked for. I had a feeling that if it was not for liability reasons, my boss would have asked me to

leave right away. Maybe it was my feeling. But my boss stopped sending me out for business meetings. Later, he explained that most of his customers come from a specific background and he was worried that my dress code would offend them. So I quit at the moment. Anyway, I was thinking of leaving my job as many of the finance practices contradicted the Islamic laws.

We must remember that the decision-making process of fundamentalists do not represent a primitive irrational mode of thinking simply because they do not fit into the paradigm of the Western rationalist approach. Rather, the fundamentalists' decisions are a product of a coherent and complex identity as influenced by the dictates of Islam and as such are not options but mandates. When it comes to issues of daily life, Islamic fundamentalists utilize a process of cost/benefit calculation as long as these decisions and goals achieved fall within the confines of the Qur'an and *Sharia*. As such, the rationalist approach does not fall outside the scope of the fundamentalist, rather, it plays a secondary role behind the mandates of the individual's identity as formed by his or her Islamic faith. The Islamic way of life takes precedence above all else, and alternatives that threaten this premise regardless of benefit are not true alternatives.

It is important to consider whether religious conversion and the subsequent decision-making processes are in any way a form of calculated self-interested behavior. Contrary to the rational choice approach, this study suggests that even if this possibility exists it is definitely unintended and that even the high costs and lack of benefit resulting from a given action is not an important factor to consider.

This brings us to the question of the extent to which these mandates are respected and whether an Islamic fundamentalist is willing to sacrifice his or her life for Islam. Each time I posed this question to the Islamic fundamentalists I interviewed, the answer was an unambiguous yes. I found that for fundamentalists, the concept of *jihad,* a holy war or struggle, is not necessarily limited to the sword; rather, every day of their life is seen as a *jihad* toward a truly righteous life. According to Rana:

> *Jihad* is something that I do every day. It is a *jihad* for Allah. It is not only fighting with arms but fighting with intelligence. Right now I am fighting for the establishment of Islam by educating people about what Islam is and that Islam is a complete way of life.

To Um Sajed, rejecting the conditions for her husband's release from Israeli prisons is *jihad*. Humbly, she responded to my inquiry about his refusal to be released and be with his family again.

No, he would not. Abu Sajed will not accept any compromise. As a Muslim, a true Muslim, he cannot but continue his struggle until all the other detainees are released. Although, we wanted him to be with us here, we agree with his decision. And you know, even when he will be released, he will continue his mission and Sajed [her son who came into the room] and all my other children will follow the path.

Benefits Are Not Intended

Islamic fundamentalists act in defense of their identity and not consciously for gain. If they express a sense of satisfaction, it is often justified as a result of following the way of Allah rather than a personal gratification based on personal gain. For Aida, Islam has helped her get over the need to satisfy life's materialistic wants and demands.

> I am no longer worried about the way I look. I am over the materialistic aspects of this life. I never thought that I will see beauty the way I see it today. I never thought that implementing every aspect of the Qur'an and Prophet Mohammad's teachings will give me the feeling of inner peace and humbleness I enjoy today.

Um Sajed continues in a similar vein in explicating the insignificance of cost in making her decision to convert:

> In middle school, I was looked down upon by my school peers and teachers because I wear the *hijab*. My teacher actually called me few times and advised me to take the *hijab* off as I am still young and tried to convince me that it is not that important. She actually thought my parents were forcing me to do this. Although I denied this, she did not believe me until she called in my parents. I am proud of wearing the *hijab* and I feel sorry for the others who look down at us.

I also asked the Shiite theologian I interviewed[19] about how his decision to convert affected his closest relationships and, after a moment of silence, he said:

> For sure it did [affect my relationships], especially my relationship with my family. They were totally against this decision. Although they were Muslims by birth, they were very liberal. [Silence] *I had to fight my way. I did not and I never will regret*

this [emphasis in the original]. I feel stronger and more self-confident today.

It is clear from these stories that Islamic fundamentalists of varying ages and from different educational and economic backgrounds make decisions and act within the boundaries of their Islamic identity as shaped by the way they think and construe the reality around them. They strive to defend the word of God and though they recognize the cost of their actions, they do not perceive it as an issue. They recognize the benefits they derive from their conversion but they perceive it as an unintended result. This is a testimony for one mode of thinking which the post-Enlightenment rationalist approach definitely fails to explain adequately.

Nonfundamentalist Calculus

The more we move away from fundamentalism on the religiosity continuum, the more we can detect a cost/benefit calculation. Whereas fundamentalists are willing to sacrifice a certain way of life or even their lives to promote God's word, nonfundamentalists are not willing to do so. In the interviews I conducted with the twenty fundamentalists, they emphasized that as long as their acts promote the word of Allah, the cost is not a question. Their example serves to clearly indicate the limitation of the post-Enlightenment rational way of thinking in explicating decisions that touch on the basic sense of self. On the other hand, the interviews I conducted with five nonfundamentalists indicate that the more we move to secularism the more calculus is detected in the subjects' decision making.

Nonfundamentalists tend to engage in cost/benefit calculations to reach decisions and set priorities. Faris who was raised in a secular environment, now ranks himself between a good and an orthodox Muslim. He says he finds it difficult to apply all the Islamic doctrines.

> Q: Since you believe sincerely in the doctrines of Islam, why don't you abide by the Islamic laws as you are supposed to do as a true Muslim?
> A: I wish I could. It is very hard. At my age [nineteen] it is not easy. I think I am not ready.
> Q: When do you think you will be ready?
> A: Maybe when I am on my own, when I have my own job. Now I am a student and I cannot let certain Islamic rules limit my progress. But later when I achieve or draw my future then I will be able to do whatever I feel right. I am not ready to pay the price now.

Moe describes himself as an engineer and a father of two boys and fits into the category of good Muslim. His attitude about Islam will likely shock the fundamentalists and presents a logic altogether foreign to a true believer. When asked about the significance of religion to him, Moe responds:

> Religion to me is a kind of an insurance. I follow the *ibadat* rituals as if I am paying my premiums. One day when the after-life comes I will be rewarded for that.

In comparing fundamentalists with nonfundamentalists, the interviews I conducted unequivocally point to a fundamentalist way of construing the world that drastically differs from that of comparable Muslim nonfundamentalists. For example, Lama identifies herself first as a mother, a wife, and a Muslim who practices the Islamic rituals. When I inquired about the fact that Islam is more than practicing the prayers and fasting, she responded:

> I know but I am not sure it answers all my questions. Life is dealing with other people, socializing, adapting to different environments. I cannot constrain myself. I have to work, earn my life, and raise my kids. I think Allah knows that I am doing the best for my family and myself. I think I will be rewarded for this in life and in heaven.

In general, nonfundamentalists reject a comprehensive and unyielding notion of religion. Although their interests are very much shaped by their respective identity, they tend to be far more involved in an individualist cost/benefit calculation.

Construals of Islamic Fundamentalists

We know no fact independent of interpretation; there is no vision of reality untainted by prejudice and perspective.
– Nietzsche, 1918

Nietzsche is right; reality is what individuals perceive and construe. But the fact that it is tainted by prejudice cannot be taken for granted especially when different perspectives collide and conflict. An understanding of the other's perspective is needed for healthier communication, unprejudiced dialogue, and conflict prevention. Having looked at some of the views of Islamic fundamentalists, nonfundamentalists, communists, and nationalists and the way they perceive themselves as individuals within their group and in relation to others, I will look at how they construe the reality they see around them.

To define this construal, I will focus on the following variables, which commonly are used when general and academic debates about fundamentalists take place. I will be looking at (1) their self-proclaimed level of religiosity, (2) their understanding of the comprehensiveness of Islam, (3) the role of reason, (4) their views on predetermination and choice, (5) their notions about truth, (6) their views on the role of science and technological advancement, (7) what they expect out of their state and leaders, (8) their interpretation of *jihad*, (9) and their views on terrorism.

Levels of Religiosity

According to our interviews, the most obvious differences between the fundamentalists, nonfundamentalists, communists and nationalists pivoted around religion. Islamic fundamentalists follow the Qur'an and the sacred laws and regulations strictly. For example, according to Imad:[20] "We are fundamentalists. We are those who follow the Qur'an without deviation. Any deviation leads to corruption. Without any doubt and with complete submission, the Qur'an and the *Sharia* are the first and last resort. I follow Islam in every aspect of life." Obeidi a fundamentalist who lives in Lebanon proclaims, "If all people follow Islam and if we have a strong Islamic state, everybody will be happy, even those who are non-Muslims." Differentiating between nonpracticing Muslims and fundamentalists, Um Sajed, a self-proclaimed fundamentalist, confirms that fundamentalists are those who with Allah's guidance they (Muslims) will then follow Islam as a way of life. Islam dictates the rules of life.

A nonfundamentalist, on the other hand, such as Fadia (a good Muslim) says, "I know that praying, fasting, and paying the alms are basic to Islamic beliefs. But truthfully, I believe they do not add anything. I am a good wife and mother." When asked whether she worries that by not abiding the mandates of God that she may be denied an entry into heaven, she responds: "Yes [replying reluctantly], but no! God knows that I am doing my duties towards my family and I will most probably be rewarded for this." When asked if this is enough to be a good Muslim, she admits, "No. I know this, but I am not ready. Maybe I am not completely convinced. To follow Islamic rituals in this world is very hard. It is not practical."

Omar (a secular Muslim) presents an extreme view of Islam. He is a businessman with one son and lives with his girlfriend. To him religion is:

> A scapegoat for people who do not want to deal with the necessities of life. I doubt that religious people can be better human beings than myself. . . . I do not think that Islam or any other religion can cover all aspects of life. I believe in life, in things that I can see and deal with. I am not selfish; I care about others and I do what I can but there are limits to what one can do.[21]

As these examples show, the level of religiosity proved to be a strong differentiating predictor between the Islamic fundamentalists and non-fundamentalists. Fundamentalists perceive all those who follow Islam in its entirety as the true Muslims while they perceive all others as corrupt, including those who claim Islam as their religion or who are born Muslims. Nonfundamentalists see themselves as good Muslims not because they follow the *Sharia* strictly but because they are good mothers, students, or citizens.

Comprehensiveness of Islam

For the fundamentalists Islamic laws and regulations shape all aspects of life: religious and moral order is the basis of all action. Islam is different from all other religions. It deals with all aspects of life. It regulates our life. "If we follow God's orders, justice will prevail," Waleed emphasizes. Nonfundamentalists reflect more the rational approach as they reject the comprehensive aspect of Islam. According to Omar, "I do not think that Islam or any other religion can cover all aspects of life."

As fundamentalists, all the interviewees agree that Islam covers all aspects of life from issues related to politics to those related to inheritance—there is absolutely no reason to ignore the mandates of Islam in practical affairs: Islam has clearly laid out the obligations of a good Muslim for all eternity. Meanwhile, nonfundamentalists see that Islam cannot cover all aspects of life and hence human initiative and reason are each extremely important. Though the fundamentalists I interviewed do not deny the significance of reason, they do see it as subservient to and always in the service of religion.

Reason Is Subservient to Religion

The failure of the rationalist approach to explain the actions of Islamic fundamentalists should not lead to the conclusion that they are irrational. In fact, all interviewees emphasized the fact that reason, logic, and mind are intrinsic aspects of the Islamic laws as specified in the Qur'an and the *Sharia*. They all voice the opinion that reason is bounded only by the words of God—or rather, that God's mandates are inherently rational and always supersede the transience of individualistic reason.

Consider Aida, a Sunnite Muslim and a mother of four who insists that everything people do is based on God's will. God gave human beings a brain to think, reason, and choose, but all is done with God's knowledge and permission. When Abdul, a thirty-nine-year-old fundamentalist and father of three children, was asked, "Between fate and hope in the afterlife, what is the status of reason in Islam?" he confidently responds:

> Of course! Mind and reason are very significant in Islam. Mind and reason are used to explain Allah's creations and to help us make right decisions. But reason cannot supercede the Text [Qur'an].

Whether Shiite or Sunnite, fundamentalists concurred on the perception of reason as subservient to faith. Sheikh Hussam a thirty-five-year-old Sunni fundamentalist, leader of the AICP, a nonmilitant Islamic social movement, repeatedly mentioned that Islam is based on reason and logic: "There is nothing in Islam that is beyond logic. Contrary to other religions that personified Allah and then crucified him, Islam showed us the truth. By using our mind we find that the ultimate truth lies in Islam."

All fundamentalists interviewed agree that reason is intrinsic to Islam. They perceive Islamic mandates as based on logic and reason that is given to humanity by God. Accordingly, individual reason can be used to better understand and explain God's creation, but not to question or undermine it.

Predetermination and Choice

Islamic fundamentalists assert that people have choices; however, they see these choices as subject to God's will. Ibraheem Musawi, a thirty-year-old Shiite fundamentalist graduate student and the press attaché of Hizbu'llah insists:

> Allah created the right and wrong and then gave us the choice. If we have strong faith then we will choose the right path and we will be rewarded. If we are not true believers then we are punished in hell. This is very important to know that every-

thing we do is predetermined by Allah. Everything is according to Allah's will. Sometimes we choose to do certain things but things that we did not intend happen. Sometimes we do not intend or want to do certain things and they happen to us. [Looking in the interviewer's eye] This is all based on Allah's will.

Aida, a Sunnite fundamentalist with a high school education and mother of four, echoes the assertions of each of the other fundamentalists: "The human being is driven by Allah's will first and foremost. Even if we plan on doing things and Allah does not will this for us then it will not happen." When asked to expand on whether she believes that *everything* is based on fate, Aida responds:

> [continuing with enthusiasm] Use your mind and tell me what do you think of this incident. . . . It was Allah's will. I left everything I was doing and decided to go to the balcony where my three-year eldest son Haitham was hanging down from the balcony's rail. I saved my son, Allah wanted me to go and save my son.

She took me to the balcony to show me how high and dangerous it was. They live in an apartment building on the fourth floor. Describing another incident where Allah seemed to determine the outcome, she explained how her family survived Israeli bombings. She knew these outcomes were in her favor because of her prayers and Allah's will. When asked if she always depends on Allah's will and leaves her fate to prayer, she remarks:

> Everything is done based on Allah's will. But Allah gave us the mind to choose between the good and bad, to do what is best for our family and people. I will not throw myself from the window and say if Allah does not will my death then I will not die. Of course we use our mind to decide on things we do every day. *But when it comes to following Allah's orders we just do it. We have to have strong faith, follow Allah's word and Mohammad's teachings* [emphasis added].

When it comes to issues that touch at the heart of their faith, Islamic fundamentalists act in defense of their identity. They say that they do not have the choice to decide among different alternatives—they are compelled by the will of God.

Science and Technological Advancement

Interestingly, most Islamic fundamentalists do not perceive of the advent of science and technology as a challenge to their ethical and religious practices. Instead, they see these advancements as tools that help human beings understand and appreciate God's creation—as the very manifestation of the qualities that differentiate human beings from other species. Most of them believe that God gave his creatures the will and ability to learn in order to reach the highest level of knowledge, along with which comes a more perfect knowledge of God's creation. They also add that the true believers use this knowledge to promote God's word. According to Sheikh:

> Science and logic are intrinsic in Islamic teachings. They [the West] try to equate us with other religions which are not logical. Allah urges us humans to learn. Allah gave us the mind to learn and the mind is a proof of Allah's creation. It is true the West is advanced technologically, but we are using this technology for the good of humanity, we use it for education, and promoting the word of Allah.

Sheikh Obeidi has a Ph.D. in Economics from the Sorbonne in Paris and has written a study on Islamic banking. Obeidi, like all the Islamic fundamentalists I interviewed, believes in science and technology when used the Islamic way.

> I am a Muslim economist; I use science, reason and mind to apply financial rules. If the West created the idea of the interest on money you save in the bank, it does not mean that this the best way to deal financially. Applying strictly Islamic banking means a healthier economy.

States and Leaders

Recognizing the fact that states and boundaries artificially separate people and nations, fundamentalists emphasize that Islam is the religion of humanity and therefore it defies boundaries. Fundamentalists identify themselves as being Muslims first and then the citizens or nationals of a certain country. Accordingly they act, adopt policies, and use Islamic laws to guide domestic and foreign relations. They perceive the obligation of statesmen as to execute and make sure that God's word is implemented in this world. The Western concept of democracy as government made by and for people collides with the Islamic fundamentalist conception of government organized to promote and apply Islamic laws and in which leaders are elected to apply these laws.

Imad, a thirty-five-year-old Sunnite fundamentalist who comes from a relatively poor family, asserts that there is no democracy in the Western sense in Islam. Democracy in Islam is the choice of a leader. The leader should be a qualified true believer who is able to execute the *Sharia* and make sure it is applied firmly. People do not have the right to change the laws of Allah. They are fixed.

Ziad, a twenty-one-year-old social science senior who comes from a middle-class Muslim family, illustrates the fundamentalist view of democracy in stating:

> In case of conflict, policy decisions should be resolved through consulting religious teachings, not political compromise. However, certain issues are not even subject to discussion. For example, the question of abortion, which is a hot issue today and a subject open to deliberations, has already been approved in some courts in the United States. But according to Islam abortion is not accepted; no matter what laws are made by man it is still *haram* [not allowed].

Islamic fundamentalists in a country such as Lebanon do function within the framework of a country where the government is organized on a sectarian basis, and in which the religious laws of each sect supplement the civil laws to govern their lives in areas such as marriage and inheritance. However, their goals and issues go beyond the nation-state. Their ultimate goal and canonical expectation continue to be the establishment of a united Islamic nation. One of the strongest concomitants of solidarity, as voiced by Sheikh Hussam, Ibrahim, and Nuha, is abiding by individual and communal responsibilities as ordained by religion and canonical law of Islam. Nuha asserts that as decreed by the prophet, help your brother whether he is the doer of wrong or wrong is done to him. And Sheikh Hussam adds, "Acts of courage, conduct of Islamic manners, and practice of sociability are the foundations of right-doing."

Jihad

To fight and die in the name of God is a duty and an honor to fundamentalist Muslims: it marks the path to heaven. Rational choice approach analysts explain the fundamentalist's decision to die in the name of God as an intended and calculated act to get the reward of heaven. But fundamentalists give a clearer explanation of *jihad*, a holy war fought in deference for and protection of God's laws. All the fundamentalists I interviewed expressed frustrations about what they perceive to be the West's unfair branding of Muslims based on misunderstood Islamic dictates such as the *jihad*. Frustrated by the Western media's tendency to brand all Muslims as terrorists, Sheikh Hussam says the Western insistence on branding Islamic fundamentalists as extremists will only lead to increased enmity from Muslims.

> Whenever an explosion or any terrorist act occurs, Islamic fundamentalists are to blame such as the Oklahoma bombing. These wrong accusations will lead to more hostility. The West should be careful that their offensive accusations bring together not only Muslims but also those who claim to be Muslims to stand against the West.

All fundamentalists agreed with the anonymous Shiite theologian that *jihad* is misinterpreted by the West.

> The Western media focuses only on the war aspect of *jihad*. However *jihad* is of two kinds. The big *jihad* is the cleansing of the soul. It is the ability to refrain from letting our instincts take over our actions. The other *jihad* is spreading the word of Allah among humanity. If any attack against Islam and Muslims is initiated, then it is our duty to fight back. Those who die are considered martyrs.

Ibraheem Musawi also voiced the fundamentalist view of the holy war. "*Jihad* is a defense and not an offense. Our duty is to defend the word of Allah and stop anything that undermines Islam."

To determine the incentives for *jihad*, I asked the interviewees to clarify the reward of heaven. The following is an excerpt from my interview with Sheikh Hussam, leader of AICP, a nonmilitant Islamic movement in Lebanon:

> Q: Those who sacrifice their life are promised heaven. Tell me more about this?
> A: Yes. Allah promised heaven to those who fight and die in his name.
> Q: So do all those who committed suicidal attacks against the Israelis automatically go to heaven?
> A.: No, not necessarily, this awaits Allah's decision. I would like also to clarify that our martyrs did not commit suicide; they sacrificed their lives to defend the word of Allah. Suicide is *haram* [not allowed].

Q: But these people die because they know that they are going
to heaven.
A: No, they do not take it for granted. They are promised but
are not necessarily going to get this reward. When they intend
to go for *jihad* they pray for Allah's will to pave their way to
heaven.[22]

   The Islamic fundamentalists statements underscore the significance
of identity in shaping attitudes and actions. A threat to Islam is a threat
to the basic identity of those who take Islam as their way of life. The sin-
gling out of Islamic fundamentalists whenever an act of terror occurs in-
furiates the fundamentalists and leads them to more extremism. The
misinterpretation and misuse of the Islamic language such as *jihad*, sui-
cide killing, and the assumption that the reward of heaven drives the Islamic believers to kill, dehumanizes Muslims and draws borders of hatred between the West and those who identify as Muslims. Definitely a
better understanding of the Islamic worldview will help Western policy
makers in dealing with Islamic fundamentalist groups and countries, if
not at least curtailing extremism.
   The ethnocentric misinterpretation and misconceptions go further to
associate Islamic fundamentalism with terrorism. This brings up the
question: What is the Islamic fundamentalists understanding of terrorism?

Terrorism

Bewildered by the international and especially the American portrayal of
Islamic fundamentalists as terrorists, the anonymous Shiite theologian
said:

> How can you or anyone with a clear brain and straight logic ac-
> cept this stereotyping? And not only stereotyping but an of-
> fense; a clear one against all Muslims. How can it be okay for
> Israelis to bomb and kill civilians and be considered the patri-
> ots while we are considered the terrorists because we are fight-
> ing for our own rights? We are fighting on our land, our occu-
> pied land.

   Sheikh Hussam furthered this defense: "What would you brand an
American soldier fighting for his land or for his country's national security?" He remained silent waiting for my answer. I returned the question
to him, "What do you call them?" He insisted that I answer. I answered:

"A martyr." He smiled, "They are martyrs and we are terrorists. Where is the justice here, where is the logic in this?"

> Q: How do you explain the events in Algeria and in Afghanistan?
> A: [Referring to the Algerian, Afghani, and similar Islamic groups] These groups claim that they are Muslims. They are not. The Algerian movements are very far from being Muslims. We as true believers are against the acts of the Algerians, the Afghanis, and the Egyptian groups. We think that these movements are hired and sponsored by those who want to taint the real Islam.

Imad agrees that what is happening in Algeria is non-Islamic. He refuses to claim anything against the Taliban because of the mixed news people get from the media and because of the direct involvement of the United States in the events, mainly their support for the rebels. However, he rejects the Western definition of terrorism and even their definition of fundamentalism.[23]

> I am not interested in the Western definition or terminology of terrorism or fundamentalism. It is only certain that each side will try to plant fear in the heart of their enemies. The West uses the same method as part of their military strategy. If threats, deterrence, and freedom fighting mean terrorism, then the tactic of terrorizing is used by different groups to deliver a message.

When I address the targeting of innocent people, Imad answers:

> A Muslim should not and cannot kill women and children, unless women are carrying arms. As far as men are concerned, they are all targets of battle. We believe that every order given by Allah in the Qur'an has a definite wisdom behind it. I am not qualified, myself to give you an explanation for the wisdom behind the order of killing a nonbeliever man and not a woman. [Pause] Nonetheless, we have to abide by Allah's scripture.

Those I interviewed were aware of the Western conception of Islamic fundamentalists as extremists, as unwilling to compromise and hence not open for dialogue. I asked the interviewees to comment on this view. According to Sheikh Hussam:

> Anyone who believes in an ideology thinks that he is right and the others are wrong. That is why we have different movements and parties. If we are branded extremists because we believe

that Islam is the only right religion, then secularists should also
be branded extremists because they believe that secularism is
right and it is the only solution to today's life and challenges.
We are open for dialogue. We are willing to communicate with
the others to persuade them that the religion of Allah is Islam
and it is the right path.

The Shiite theologian continues in a similar vein:

> We are not against dialogue. We are not afraid to open com-
> munication with the West. I think they are. [He looked at me
> and proceeded to challenge me to get him a visa to the United
> States to come and spread the true word of Allah.]

Even Imad, the most militant and demonstrative in showing his dis-
satisfaction with the Western policies toward Muslims, disclosed his
readiness, however reserved, to cooperate with the West.

When asked if he sees any possible cooperation with the West, he responds:

> Yes, of course. There can be trade and treaties. We need the
> technology of the West because we still lack our own. But at the
> same time, we should be very careful in our dealings with the
> West because they only give us what will weaken us and do not
> contribute to our progress. We need to interact with the West-
> ern societies in order to show them the true version of Islam
> and not the Western propaganda version.

In sum, to the fundamentalist whose basic identity overarches all
other identities and dictates all aspects of life, public as well as private,
the Western conception of Islamic fundamentalists as terrorists is a
skewed vision of Islam and Islamic concepts.

Conclusion

In my analysis, I argue that cognition is influenced by norms and culture.
Norms are internalized through socialization; this cultural component of
socialization is then reflected in the actor's particular cognitive constructions and construals. Culture helps shape the human mind and gives
meaning to action. The particular way in which this occurs for an individual will be reflected through the patterns embedded in the culture's
symbolic systems, in its language and discourse modes and in the forms
of logical and narrative explication.[24]

Fundamentalists are those who follow the Qur'an without deviation. To a secular Muslim on the left side of my continuum religion is a scapegoat for people who do not want to deal with the necessities of life. Nonfundamentalists reject the idea that religion can cover all aspects of life. Nonfundamentalists agree that religion offers certain ethical guidelines but scriptures written fourteen centuries ago cannot deal with today's problems.

In deciphering the construals, I confirm the view that there is a gap between the Islamic fundamentalist and the Western worldview. The Islamic fundamentalists interests are not perceived as interests but rather as moral imperatives. Moreover, the interest of the Islamic fundamentalist is not to maximize self-interest but the destiny and moral conditions of the entire community. I argue that a better understanding of the way the Islamic fundamentalists perceive and interpret reality helps provide a tool for dialogue. Islamic fundamentalists, contrary to the Western assumptions, are ready for dialogue. The Shiite theologian voiced the opinion of all fundamentalists: "We are not against dialogue. We are not afraid to open communication with the West. I think they are." Moreover, Islamic fundamentalists believe that the Western stigmatization of all Islamic movements as extremists, backward, irrational, and terrorists make the Islamic fundamentalists feel backed into the corner and hence aggressive. Sheikh Hussam, the leader of the AICP, a moderate Islamic movement, discloses that these wrong accusations will lead to more hostility. The West should be careful that their offensive accusations bring together not only Muslims but also those who claim to be Muslims to stand against the West.

In summary, I argue that Western governments that wish to initiate a fruitful discourse with Islamic fundamentalists need a clear understanding of what is required, an understanding that is based on the fact that Islamic fundamentalists have a different cognitive worldview and that they act in defense of their basic identity. My analysis provides a portrait of Islamic fundamentalists in which their Islamic identity dictates all aspects of their lives. Islamic fundamentalism reflects a belief in which the private and public overlap, the ultimate truth is the divine truth and reason is shaped by faith, allegiance to the Qu'ran as the supreme law.

This narrative analysis can serve as a prelude to further studies that will lead to a better understanding of all religious fundamentalism. The use of social identity and construals can also be utilized to compare Islamic fundamentalism with Christian and Jewish fundamentalism.[25]

Since this study deals with moderate and militant Islamic fundamentalists in Lebanon who have some political power either as representatives in the government and/or act independently by providing social and welfare services,[26] I suggest that a narrative analysis could be utilized to decipher the construals of Islamic fundamentalists already in power and to test whether the identity of the Islamic fundamentalists shifts depending on the position of power each individual holds. For this purpose, a study of Islamic fundamentalism in Iran is an example of Islamic fundamentalists in power.[27]

One of the lessons to be learned from this narrative analysis is that a different perspective is needed. My analysis provides a political psychology approach with a focus on social identity and the effects of construals. The narrative utilized in this study delineates the way Islamic fundamentalists interpret the reality they see around them: the decisions and actions of the members of both the moderate and militant Islamic movements are constrained by their Islamic identity. Their Islamic identity is a core identity which overarches all other identities and which reflects a belief in which the line between the private and public is blurred, the ultimate truth is in the word of God, and reason is subservient to faith.

Notes

1. Islam presents a critique of other ideologies. Islamic resurgence is presented as a return to the righteous path as an alternative to westernization whether depicted in communism, and/or capitalism. The return to Islam is the return to a divinely order where faith directs human reason.

2. The perception of fundamentalist Islam as a menace has evolved for over two centuries and has been illustrated by different reactions and accusations. The Western stereotyping and belief that Islamic revival constitutes a threat is well described in Esposito's study *The Islamic Threat: Myth or Reality*, 1993. To expand on the causes and origins of the Western conceptions and misperceptions is well beyond the scope of this study.

3. John Esposito in his books *Islam and Politics* (1984) and *Islamic Threat: Myth or Reality* (1995) and Samuel Huntington in his study *The Clash of Civilizations: Remaking of World Order* (1996) each focus on the cultural differences between the West and Islamic fundamentalists and the effect of such disparity on an individual's respective perspective.

4. Iannaccone (1990) treats religion as a household commodity: consumers choose religion after they calculate the respective costs and benefits involved. These household goods can be categorized as experience goods versus search goods. Religion is a kind of commodity which can be assessed in line with personal experience but he insists that this is achieved with greater difficulty than that of other commodities, such as used cars. Therefore institutions are required to facilitate and provide information.

5. Marty and Appleby, 1991; Sahliyeh, 1991; Yafeh, 1988; Misztel and Shupe, 1992; Swatos, 1989; Robertson and Chirico, 1985. Phebe Marr, "The United States, Europe, and the Middle East: An Uneasy Triangle," *Middle East Journal* 48, (1994) 224. Cf. Hilal Khashan, 1991.

6. See Chouieri, 1997; Dobbin, 1983; Habib, 1978; Ziadeh, 1968.

7. See Adams, 1968; Ahmad, 1967; Gibb, 1975; Kerr, 1966; Keddie, 1972; Noer, 1973.

8. See Esposito, 1984; Picatori, 1991.

9. Monroe and Kreidie, 1997, 19.

10. *Ident.*

11. Lewin, 1948; Heider, 1958; Festinger, 1980.

12. Monroe, 1995.

13. Cf. Monroe and Kreidie, 1997.

14. *Ident.*

15. Monroe and Kreidie, 1997, 19

16. Monroe and Kreidie, 1997, 35.

17. He identified himself as a secular born Muslim. He is a thirty-five-year-old businessman and lives with his girl friend. Omar comes from a middle-class family. He moved from Jordan to the United states at age eighteen, got his degree in business, and since then he has been involved in the gold mining business.

18. As mentioned on p. 139, interviewees were put on a continuum from secular on the extreme left to fundamentalist on the extreme right with mainstream (labeled themselves as good) and orthodox Muslims in the center.

19. This interviewee is one of the security officials of Hizbu'llah who wanted to keep his identity anonymous.

20. The interviews were conducted between 1995 and 1996. I kept in touch with almost all of them. University students are working now. Imad has moved from Lebanon to the United States and is working as a religious educator and leader. He is married to a European and Islamic convert woman whom he met while in Germany. Nuha is still teaching Islamic studies to people of different ages. The anonymous interviewee is still in a leadership position today and his Islamic group AICP is among the largest fundamentalist Sunnite groups in Beirut. May is now married to a fundamentalist and a mother of two. I lost track of Ziad and Waleed. I was told that Waleed went back to Egypt.

21. Monroe and Kreidie, 1997, 38.

22. As a side-note, Islamic fundamentalists also offered a different interpretation of the death of a martyr. Martyrs are not considered dead and their bodies will not disintegrate. Um Sajed explains that martyrs are not considered dead but alive and under Allah's grace. She, along with all others I interviewed, repeat the same Qur'anic verse: "And say not of those who are slain in the way of Allah: They are dead. Nay, they are living, though you perceive (it) not" (Qur'an 2:54). To illustrate how this works, she told the story of her brother who was killed in a battle. After his death, he was around them all the time and only her father and herself were able to see him physically. He would talk to them but not to his grandmother because she was mourning his death and this is against the teaching of Islam. Imad confirms this concept of death, "the words of the Qur'an are very bold and clear. The Qur'an says that the bodies of the people who have died in battle in the name of Allah will not disintegrate for eternity." As a proof, Imad also tells this story:

> For example, one radio station reporter saw that the bodies of the Afghan fighters did not dissolve or disintegrate, even after remaining for days in the sun, while those of the Russian soldiers did and the Russian poured acid on the Afghan bodies for

the sake of the Russian soldiers' morale.

23. At the start of the interview, I had to explain my definition of fundamentalism as the strict adherence to the Qur'an and *Sharia*. At his suggestion of using true believer as substitute for fundamentalist, I had to clarify my use of the term, explaining it was necessary to use a target word that Westerners readily utilize.

24. This makes the interpretation of a narrative a powerful tool for understanding the different ways in which culture influences behavior.

25. I suggest Christian and Jewish religions because these religions, like Islam, trace their religious tradition to the one true God. The Judeo-Christian and Muslim monotheism share an Abrahamic faith with its common belief in God, prophets, revelation, a divinely ruled community, and moral responsibility. (Voll 1983).

26. In 2000, Hizbu'llah had four representatives in the parliament. The AICP had two in the previous parliament terms. The Islamic group ran twice for elections but did not get any seats in the parliament.

27. Today, Iran is the most successful example of an Islamic fundamentalist nation governed by Mullahs (Shiite religious sheikhs and theologians). Saudi Arabia is an Islamic nation but not governed by theologians.

References

Adams, Charles. *Islam and Modernism in Egypt: A Study of the Modern Reform Movement Inaugurated by Muhammad `Abduh*. New York: Russell & Russell 1968.

Ahmad, Khurshid (ed.). *Islam: Its Meaning and Message*. Foreword by Salem Azzam. London: Islamic Council of Europe, distributed by News and Media, 1976.

Chouieri, Yousef. M. *Islamic Fundamentalism*. London: Pinter, 1997.

Dobbin, Christine. *Islamic Revivalism in a Changing Peasant Economy: Central Sumatra, 1784–1847*. London: Curzon Press, 1983.

Esposito, John. *Islam and Politics,* 1st ed. Syracuse, N.Y.: Syracuse University Press, 1984.

———. *Islamic Threat: Myth or Reality*. New York: Oxford University Press, 1995.

Festinger, Leon (ed.). *The Retrospection of Social Psychology*. Oxford: Oxford University Press, 1980.

Gibb, H. A. R. *Mohammedanism: An Historical Survey*. London: Oxford University Press, 1979.

Habib, Boularès. *Nous Partons pour la Tunisie*. Paris: Jean Duvignaud, PUF, 1978.

———. *Islam: The Fear and the Hope*. Atlantic Highlands, NJ: Zed Books, 1990.

Heider, Fredrick. *The Psychology of Interpersonal Relations*. New York: Wiley, 1958.

Huntington, Samuel P. *The Clash of Civilizations and the Remaking of World Order*. New York: Simon & Schuster, 1996.

Iannaccone, L. R. Religious Participation: A Human Capital Approach, *Journal for the Scientific Study of Religion* 29, no. 3 (1990): 297–314.

Jansen, G. H. *Militant Islam*. New York: Harper & Row, 1979.

Keddie, N. R. Ideology, "Sociology and the State in Post-Colonial Muslim Societies," *States and Ideology in the Middle East and Pakistan,* Fred Halliday and Alavi Hamza (eds.). New York: Monthly Review Press, 1988.

Kerr, M. H. *Islamic Reform: the Political and Legal Theories of Muhammad `Abduh and Rash'id Rid'a*. Berkeley, CA: University of California Press, 1966.

Khashan, H. "The New World Order and the Tempo of Militant Islam," paper presented at the 18th Summer International School on Disarmament and Research on Conflicts course, Certosa di Pontignano, Italy, July 29, 1996.

Lewin, K. "Resolving Social Conflicts," *Selected Papers in Group Dynamics.* New York: Harper, 1948.

Marty, M. E., and R. S. Appleby (eds.). *Fundamentalisms Observed: A Study Conducted by the American Academy of Arts and Sciences.* Chicago: University of Chicago Press, 1991.

Misztel, B., and A. Shupe (eds.). *Religion and Politics in Comparative Perspective: Revival of Religious Fundamentalism in East and West.* Westport, CT: Praeger, 1992.

Monroe, K. "But What Else Could I Do? Choice, Identity, and a Cognitive Perceptual Theory of Ethical Behavior," *Political Psychology* 15, no. 1 (1995): 201–226.

Monroe, K., and L. H. Kreidie. "The Perspectives of Islamic Fundamentalism and the Limits of Rational Choice Theory," *Political Psychology* 18, no. 1 (1997): 19–42.

Piscatori, J. *Islamic Fundamentalisms and the Gulf Crisis*. Fundamentalism Project, The American Academy of Arts and Sciences, Chicago, IL, 1991

Robertson, R., and J. Chirico. "Humanity, Globalization, and Worldwide Religious Resurgence: A Theoretical Exploration," *Sociological Analysis* 46 (1985): 219–59.

Sahliyeh, E. (ed.). *Religious Resurgence and Politics in the Contemporary World*. Albany: State University of New York Press, 1991.

Swatos, W. H. Jr. *Religious Politics in Global and Comparative Perspective*. New York: Greenwood Press, 1989.

Yafeh, H. L. "Contemporary Fundamentalism: Judaism, Christianity, Islam," *Jerusalem Quarterly* 47 (1988): 27–39.

Ziadeh, F. J. *Lawyers, the Rule of Law and Liberalism in Modern Egypt.* Stanford, CA: Hoover Institution on War, Revolution, and Peace, Stanford University, 1968.

Index

About the Contributors

Robert Coles, Professor of Psychiatry and Medical Humanities at Harvard University, is the Pulitzer Prize-winning author of more than fifty books. Coles is best known for his explorations of children's moral, political, and spiritual sensibilities in the five-volume *Children of Crisis* series and the three-volume *The Inner Life of Children* series. Among his biographical writings is *Erik Erikson: The Growth of His Work* (1970). Coles is a columnist for *The New Republic, New Oxford Review, American Poetry Review*, and is the editor of *DoubleTake Magazine*. In 1988, he received the nation's highest civilian honor, The Medal of Freedom, from President Clinton.

Lena Klintbjer Ericksen, Lecturer in Psychology, Western Washington University, did graduate work in the University of Chicago's program on Human Development. Among her instructors was Erik Erikson. She received her Ph.D. at the University of California–Davis. She teaches courses in human development and the politics of identity.

Lawrence Friedman, Professor of History, Indiana University, is the author of *Identity's Architect: A Biography of Erik Erikson* (1999), as well as *Menninger: The Family and the Clinic* (1992). His writings include psychological studies, biographical analysis, and intellectual history. The recipient of four NEH fellowships, he held the Fulbright Distinguished Chair to Germany for 2001-02, and is International Author of the Year for 2003, selected by the International Biographical Society of Cambridge. Prof. Friedman is an activist for the rights of minorities, scholars, and the mentally ill.

Kenneth Hoover, Professor of Political Science, Western Washington University, is the author of *Economics as Ideology: Keynes, Laski, Hayek and the Creation of Contemporary Politics* (2003). The book employs identity relations analysis to examine the link between identity formation and the creation of ideologies. He has written five other books, all of which deal with relationships between identity and topics such as ideology, normative political theory, and the uses and misuses of methodology. See http://www.ac.wwu.edu/~khoover/.

Catarina Kinnvall, Assistant Professor of Political Science at Lund University, Sweden, is the author of *Globalization and the Construction of Identity: Democracy, Diversity and Nationhood in India* (forthcoming), and the coeditor of *Globalization and Democratization in Asia: The Construction of Identity* (2002). She analyzes relationships between globalization, identity, and democratic movements in Asia and shows how global-local linkages may be constructed in various ways and produce a number of different results depending on context. She is currently writing a book, *In the Name of Tradition: Globalization and Dislocation in Postcolonial Societies*, on globalization, religion, nationalism, and gender in India.

Lina Haddad Kreidie, Lecturer at the University of California–Irvine, completed her Ph.D. in Political Science in 2000. She led a project over several years of interviewing Islamic fundamentalists in Lebanon and the U.S.. She has co-authored with Kristen Renwick Monroe, "Psychological Boundaries and Ethnic Conflict: How Identity Constrained Choice and Worked to Turn Ordinary People into Perpetrators of Ethnic Violence during the Lebanese Civil War," in the *International Journal Of Politics, Culture and Society* 16, no. 1 (Fall 2002).

Jane Kroger, Professor of Psychology, University of Tromsø, Norway, has devoted her career to the study of the identity formation process in adolescent and adult development. Her recent works include *Identity Development: Adolescence through Adulthood* (2000), and articles on structural dimensions of the ego identity statuses, cross-cultural studies of identity formation, the measurement of resiliency in identity maintenance, gender and identity, and a book on *Identity in Adolescence: The Balance between Self and Other*, 2cd ed. (1996).

James Marcia, Professor Emeritus of Clinical/Developmental Psychology, Simon Fraser University, is the developer of the Identity Status Interview, a benchmark analytical tool in the study of identity formation that has been widely used by psychologists in a variety of cultural settings. He has summarized these studies in *A Handbook for Psychosocial Research* (1993) among numerous other works. He and his colleagues in various universities around the world have used this tool to expand and validate Erikson's principal construct as well as some critical derivative concepts.

Kristen Renwick Monroe, Professor of Political Science at the University of California–Irvine and Director of the Program in Political Psychology, is the author of several books including *The Heart of Altruism* (Princeton, 1996), which was awarded the 1997 Best Book Award by the American Political Science Association Section in Political Psychology and nominated for the Pulitzer Prize. Her recent work, *A Different Way of Seeing Things: Moral Choice during the Holocaust*, concerns identity and moral choice. She is a former vice president of the American Political Science Association and Director of the UCI Interdisciplinary Center for the Scientific Study of Ethics and Morality.